UNDER AND
UP AGAIN

Under and Up Again

Edith Noordewier Foley

Library of Congress Control Number:		2009910077
ISBN:	Hardcover	978-1-4415-7394-0
	Softcover	978-1-4415-7393-3

To order additional copies of this book, contact:
Xlibris Corporation
1-888-795-4274
www.Xlibris.com
Orders@Xlibris.com
66207

ACKNOWLEDGEMENTS

I am grateful to Anne Sirna for showing me how writing should and can be

to Syd Thayer Bortner for making the first adjustments

to Gail Johnston for her encouragement and knowledge

to Virginia Catherwood and Bill Turpin for their gentle criticism and guidance during our weekly writing get-togethers

to Hilde Schulze Arndt and Ingeborg Burgers Teipe who are always close although living far away

to Horst von Bassewitz to relive Kartzow and Ina Sonntag to revive it

to my sister Micaela who suffered more than she knows

1

The song was jubilant in the quiet of the early morning dawn. The window of the children's room was open to let in the fresh air, which was gently moving the sheer curtains. The bird sang and sang. I was fascinated by the melody of its song, amazed by the strength of sound produced by such a small creature. I watched and listened, lying in my bed in the stillness of the sleeping household and it made me happy. The bird sat in the same spot every morning on the flat light gray roof of the building facing us across a grass courtyard, part of our Berlin apartment complex that was located on the street that stretched from the heart of town out to the woods and lakes Berlin was so well-known for.

A park visible from our top-floor apartment known as the Lietzensee Park played a large role in my life. My mother insisted that I was taken every day for a walk there for at least one hour. These walks in my early childhood were filled with beauty and joy. We looked at the swans to see whether they had their dark gray cygnets following them, dobbering behind their parents, swimming proudly on the lake. When I got too close to see them better, the parent swans would, as a warning, unfold their wings slightly.

We could rent a rowboat and paddle from the main lake to a connecting lake by passing under a bridge. The grass so well tended with many benches on its borders to rest on, to look at the flowerbeds. Willows on the edge of the lake dipped their hanging branches into the water. A lifelike statue of Venus stood in a small circle formed by a path. The statue looked very elegant and peaceful, holding her hand coyly to her face. The nannies pushing their baby carriages. The playgrounds and the handsome statues of classical maidens. We took bread along to feed the ducks.

Some of the bushes smelled delicious in the spring and produced white round fruits that were fun to crush between my fingers. They popped.

In the winter, one of the grass fields had enough of a slope to sled down, and the lakes froze over, enough to be opened for ice-skating.

Many nights, in the dark, out of the safety of my bed, I could hear lively conversation on the balcony. My parents and maybe four or five of their friends sat there comfortably amongst the oleanders in large pots and the red geraniums cascading along the railings of the banister. A lamp with a parchment shade provided light. Their banter and laughter came often and made me feel happy and secure. This was a happy peaceful time—little did any of us suspect what the future held in store.

2

Next door across the stairway hall lived the Griebens. Tante Dodo and Tante Käthe Stein provided a lot of fun for their niece and nephew Leonie and Gerd. Leonie was older than I, and Gerd, younger. Gerd had a great sense of humor. The joy was the *Kasperle Spiele*, which are classical German marionette plays, done by the aunties, to which I was always invited. Kasperle is the main character getting into all sorts of trouble, and we children loved it. When it was over, sending me back home across the hallway, the aunties—always first with clenched teeth—squeezed my cheeks and found me adorable. "Look at her hands, she has dimples on them." referring to my knuckles. They enjoyed telling a story about me. It turned out that when I had an accident, I would stick my wet panties into their mailbox so that my mother would not find out.

When I returned home, across the hallway, my mother always wanted to know whether the Griebens had asked any questions. I was five years old, an age when it was natural to show off what had been heard: "My mother says . . ." or "My father says . . ." The year is 1935 and we are in Berlin Germany, where Hitler, already in power, is promising prosperity to the German people who are having a hard time after the peace treaty of the First World War. Poverty and hunger was their way of life. His rise to power became dangerous to those who, in any way, doubted him. We never knew who were Nazis who would report us, which was expected, and would bring kudos to those who did the reporting. Times are starting to change. Many of our neighbors and friends are disappearing or suddenly leaving.

I enjoyed the happy Markuses. The father had painted a teakettle into my "Poesie" album with a person in it blowing out steam. It said, "When you are up to your neck in hot water, do as the kettle and sing." Their move made me sad. They had been so sophisticated in a humorous way.

3

Our household runs on a schedule with little change. My father, the foreign correspondent in Berlin of a prominent Dutch newspaper the *Nieuwe Rotterdamsche Courant*, has a PhD in the Dutch language, which was a requisite to work for this paper. He started his job in 1924 in Berlin, writing a syndicated column translated into eleven languages. When his time came to take on the position of editor back at Rotterdam headquarters in Holland, the management of the paper asks him to stay on because of his invaluable

insight into the political developments in Germany at that time. Our home then also becomes the place where correspondents from other European newspapers come to hear what Father has to say. They are a lusty group with a great sense of humor. Cigar smoking is in. They meet at least once

a week or whenever something important had to be reviewed. Under the circumstances, they all become real good friends. I remember them still. Once in a while, I was allowed to do my curtsy to them.

Father writes his article in his workroom. Shelves filled with books line the wall with brown velvet panels sliding over them. On top is a collection of string instruments Father collects—balalaikas and such. Deep leather chairs, a sofa and a low round table stand in the middle of the room and two writing desks. For a while, there is a secretary by the name of Kurt Weill. Kurt Weill was a famous German composer; he was a Jew and therefore in danger at that time in Germany. Hitler starts to eliminate all Jews. I learn later that Father was active in rescuing Jews by smuggling them and their portable possessions out of Germany to Holland with the help of a Dutch friend who traveled back and forth by train between Holland and Germany. This is how Fritz Kreisler's violin made it out of Germany, and many paintings rolled up and thrown behind the suitcase on the luggage rack above the train seat. Kurt Weill, in his role of Father's secretary, is seated at another desk on the other side of Father's study, with the painted portrait of a Noordewier forefather. All of Father's articles are cut out of the newspaper and neatly glued on to pages in big books.

In 1935 Queen Wilhelmina bestows the order of Ridder of Oranje Nassau on him.

On Vati's desk are brass replicas of a discus thrower and a hound. I have the hound now here in front of me, a powerful reminder of my childhood with my father. The article he writes during the day has to be dictated by phone to the paper in Rotterdam at 12:30 AM every night. Mother waits for him to finish in the living room, with a martini for him and herself. She has been embroidering or knitting to bide the time. This late-night hour makes it necessary for Father to take a nap every afternoon. The entire household shuts down to make that possible. Everybody naps.

4

I have a photo of my father and me walking in the park, a rare occasion, very much enjoyed by me. Vati is walking with his usual walking stick, which he gaily swings up between each step, and I push a doll carriage with my black—yes, black—baby doll in it. We are making a point here. The doll is definitely not Aryan—Hitler's ideal of a pure race.

I have little interest in game toys. One game I received as a present, considered to be rather sophisticated for that time, is a board with questions and a choice of metal buttons next to them. When touching the correct answer with a metal wand, a light lights on. Well, I soon figure out that when you slide the wand over all the metal buttons, one is bound to light up. So that is that for an intellectual challenge.

I love to read. Somehow, we have a good selection of fairy tales: Grimm, Hans Christian Andersen, Hauff, Gottheil, and Selma Lagerlöf, who with her tales of the boy traveling on the backs of wild geese explored all of Sweden. This gives me a sense that animals are living a life of their own. That realization has never left me.

The pictures and drawings in the fairy tale books fascinate me. Some are dark and a bit threatening. I am about eight years old when my father gives me my first novel. It is a teenage-type story where, at the happy ending, the boy said, "Amo, ama, amamat." I was surprised, enjoyed it and was sure that my dad must have made a mistake; it was so adult. Right after that, I received Schwab's *Die Sagen des Klassischen Altertums*, Greek mythology. At a later time in another house, totally by accident and since nobody pays any attention to what I am doing, I find the entire *One Thousand and One Nights* and read them all. I am eleven at that time. I am not shocked nor surprised, which proves that young children will only absorb what they can handle.

5

My grandfather was a farmer in Pomerania. He and his wife had seven children. Mother, the youngest, and I went to visit several times. We are picked up from the rail station by horse and buggy by my uncle Herrmann. I was fascinated by the movement of the horses, their broad backs moving in the rhythm of their trotting. Their smell was the first sign of farm life.

Help with chores was always needed, and I learned how tough it is to work on a farm. Cows, horses, pigs and chickens, all in separate stables. The smell is pungent. They all have to be fed. Potatoes are boiled in large pots and then cut up with a handheld masher. That smells delicious, and I love to help feed the pigs. Milking cows fascinates me. It is done by hand by an aunt sitting on a three-legged stool, with her bandannad forehead resting on the flank of the cow. Once in a while, a cow will swish its tail over the head of the milker. The straight stream of the milk noisily hits the bucket in a steady rhythm. This is not just milk. There is cream rising to the surface and sitting on top to be made into butter in a closed wooden bucket with a plunger. When pushed up and down, it eventually produces sweet yellow butter. The residue of this activity is refreshing buttermilk to drink. But wait—from the buttermilk, they make cheese by placing it in a linen piece of cloth to separate the water from the solids, boiling it and then letting it do its thing in the linen cloth hung up in a cool spot to become a strong-tasting cheese.

Hay has to be cut with a long sickle by the men—a regular, broad, swinging motion. The grain, still on its stalks, is then picked up by armfuls and bound together into sheaves, then dried in the field by making them lean against each other.

Riding through the countryside, the standing bunches in regular rows are pretty. When the moment is right, they are brought in by horse-drawn wooden wagons with large wheels. A threshing machine separates the grain. Hay is piled with tongued forks into the barn. My uncle stands on top and disappears from sight as he gets higher and higher; the hay reaches up to the loft.

The straw to keep the animals comfortable and dry derives from the stems of the grain. The grain itself is fodder for the horses, cows and chickens and for making flour for baking bread.

Lupines, bright blue flowers coming up in the spring in the fields, are grown to replace the minerals to the soil as a fertilizer, another pleasant thing to see.

Everybody goes out to harvest sugar beets in the fields in the late fall. They are pulled out of the earth by hand while stooping down. It is cold, and gloves protect against it and the rough surface of the beets. Food and drink in enamel canisters are taken along to be consumed during the one-time rest period everyone takes at the same time. Pulling the beets is a very hard work—they are the size of a small cantaloupe—and also the work that comes afterwards. The beets are cut up then boiled for a very long time and become brown molasses, which is used as a sweetening agent or put on bread. No, not on a slice of bread first covered with butter. That was considered to be a double luxury.

Bread baking is a village affair. The village is built in a circle with a lake in the middle and also a brick oven the size of a small garden shack. Here, the breads are baked, another lengthy procedure. A piece of sourdough is saved at each occasion from bread baking to bread baking. Rye flour, water and the sourdough piece are incorporated by kneading it in a wooden trough about the size of a small bathtub. Much kneading by hand is required to make bread dough ready for baking. Finally, the breads are formed into loaves about fifteen inches long and seven inches wide and five inches high, and taken to the village oven. Their crust becomes dark brown with white flower clinging to it, one has to really chew hard eating it.

Breakfast was important to make energy for the forthcoming work in the fields. Porridge made of oatmeal without sugar, a slice of the bread with molasses on it. I remember liverwurst with pieces of meat in it and a spicy sausage made of blood and pieces of fat and sage eaten at lunch. We are not allowed to eat when there is a thunderstorm, which indicates that God is not pleased. The table is scrubbed wood, which is white. So is the floor with handmade hooked rugs here and there for color and warmth. I am fascinated with my grandfather, sitting across from me at the table having a meal, a sturdy man who rarely spoke, of average height, sinewy, with a mustache. My uncles make up for this man's severity with their jokes, teasing and laughter. There is no grandmother; she had died when I was too young to remember her.

Warm meals are prepared in the kitchen—a small room, dark, with no windows, brick flooring and a stove fueled with sticks of wood. Once the fire has really taken hold, a brick of pressed coal is added. Pots are heavy and black with soot on the outside because they sit directly on the fire. The opening for the pots can be made larger or smaller to fit the size of the pot by removing iron rings with a hook. Looking up, there is a hole in the ceiling. Long smoked sausages and hams hang in the attic. Consequently, I think, my grandmother died of lung cancer.

To slaughter a pig is a difficult affair. It is done with a large pointed knife. My uncle has to do that. Mother and I are in the living room the farthest away from the scene. I bury my head in mother's lap to drown out the screaming of the pig. The knife has to be plunged just right, and I think my uncle has a hard time doing this.

The pig has many parts to it that keep the family nourished throughout time, starting with the blood that is drained from the animal's body by hanging it up by its feet. I remember that and the making of sausages. The meat mixture is driven into pieces of entrails that first have to be emptied then boiled to sanitize them. The blood is used to make a spicy blood sausage and the liver sausage has whole pieces of liver and fat in it. I help with the stuffing. The meat smells of herbs of oregano and garlic.

The killing of animals, which is part of farm life, I cannot handle well. A chicken's body keeps moving after its head is cut off. The feathers are plucked and the stubbles singed over a flame. I still can smell the odor. Then the entrails are taken out. A chicken is also full of eggs inside, little yellow balls. This is all so terrible.

Remember, I am brought up with fairy tales and a park with swans and statues of beautiful maidens. Now in my life, it takes very little for me to not want to eat meat.

There is no running water in the house. An outside pump needs to be cranked by hand, and water buckets are brought inside. To wash, water is poured into deep porcelain bowls adorned with flowered patterns. Under each bed stands a porcelain chamber pot. The toilet was outside, way down a path, reached by walking through the vegetable and flower garden. A small wooden shack with a hole cut into a seat to sit over, open to the outside air. It is so cold and windy that the natural urges usually stop. Paper is hanging on a hook to use, unfortunately a cut-up magazine or something with shiny pages.

The living room has a wooden framed bed hidden behind a curtain. White handspun linen covers the goose-down pillows and the featherbed, which is in the shape of a pillow large enough to cover a person and thick enough to keep the person warm. All linen is handspun, also the towels. It is coarse and nubbly but amazingly fine.

In the living room is the spinning wheel. Wool from the sheep, after being washed, is spun into yarn to knit warm sweaters. How marvelous; a formless clump turns into a thread by pushing with the foot on a wooden plank to make a wheel turn. This turns a clump of wool to a desired thickness of thread. Mother tells me that she is not allowed to just knit or just read; both activities have to be done at the same time. I always have liked the clicking of knitting needles.

On the white scrubbed wooden floors lie colorful braided rugs made from discarded cotton clothing and there are lace curtains covering the three small windows. All this, a powerful example on how to depend on oneself, which reaches into my life as a reminder to, when necessary, do more than expected. I consider the handwoven linen sheet I inherited a treasure.

6

My aunts and one uncle live in or near Berlin and are a steady support system. At the Sunday church service, now I include my uncle Ernst in the prayers of the departed. He was my favorite person while growing up as a child. He radiated lightheartedness. His handsome face lit up with a smile when he saw me, and he considered what I was doing important enough to participate. Mutti did not; she was too unsure of herself. We sat down at a table and he explained to me how to cover a schoolbook with the bright  blue shiny paper that was used at the time. He carefully creased the sides where the cover would be and folded the edges just so. I still use the then-learned skill when wrapping Christmas gifts and when sewing with fancy material.

He worked for Herr Wiegand, a well-known designer of men's wear for years and then decided to start his own firm. Herr Wiegand had his business on the Witzlebenstrasse in an elegant apartment building close to us. Onkel Ernst moved to a street-front location some side streets away. When approaching his place, we could hear him whistle a cheery

tune. He sat on top of a large cutting table with his legs crossed, always glad to see us. Everybody liked him, and he was always happy. He was a good-looking man, tall, slim and with a friendly face. He found himself a pretty wife. Soon they had a baby, a little girl. The war was in full swing, and Onkel Ernst was drafted. The next thing I remember is that he visited us and he showed us a bullet hole in his cap. He had been in Greece and other places with the army and was actually used more for troop support in the uniform repair unit than for front fighting. That relieved us. We looked in on his bride and his baby, named Doris, who was growing up in the working place—very small and not really suitable for a family. Once in a while we would find the baby all alone with the mother gone. The life became too difficult for her to handle. Her grandmother took over, and the four aunts stood by.

Onkel Ernst managed to survive in the German army. I think he knew how to outsmart regulations. The last time we saw him, to everyone's consternation, he had an SS insignia on his otherwise normal green army uniform. He and we were appalled. He had been drawn into that department probably to sew and repair the uniforms of the big shots.

At the end of the war in 1945, he was in the east of Germany with troops withdrawing to the west. Not too far from Berlin, close to Stettin, he was killed.

All those years, and he should die at the end of the war. It still hurts. In my mind I hear his voice, his whistling and his laughter. The easygoing man, my Onkel Ernst.

7

It is 1935. I am now five years old. We have traveled from Berlin and are at the Baltic Sea for the summer. A house has been rented; mother, my sister and the maid are there. I am charmed by a white bear, a person who, dressed as a bear, poses with tourists for photos. I love that bear.

The Baltic Sea has no tides; the sand is a beautiful beige. Wooden walking planks lead through grass from the street to the beach. A colorful beach basket gives shelter against the chilly wind blowing in from the Russian east or the Scandinavian north. The beach basket is a handy movable device with an upholstered bench for two to sit on—with drawers underneath to put away gear and a movable roof against whatever nature has in mind. I like their colorfulness dotting the beach.

Since it is chilly and the wind is always blowing, I dig a large hole in the sand to sit in just for myself. I call it the fort. Father comes and visits. He walks down to the beach where we are, dressed in a linen suit. Linen wrinkles something awfully.

Exercise class on the beach is a routine. A lithesome blond lady, who I knew as Tante Käthe, has a handheld drum she beats rhythmically with the leather ball attached to the end of a stick and tells us to stretch and bend and then some. There are no shells on the edge of the ocean, but there are old fir tree woods in the area and this is where amber is found.

8

Father has the most amazing cars over time. We ride, with an open roof, something very new and sporty—a beige Röhr Junior. Later I remember that he has a wine red Hanomag made in Czechoslovakia, I hear.

Why am I so afraid of being in and on moving things? I am in a photo, on a tricycle, protesting against having to ride the thing; you can see it on my face that I am really angry. I am disgusted. It was almost impossible to get me first into father's car. I have no idea. It will come to me. I did get over it.

Mother, my father, and I take rides into the German countryside in the car. All is very easily reached in Europe—the distances between landscapes and their characteristics like mountains and valleys and flat fields with wide rivers, waterfalls and picturesque small towns are short. As we stop for lunch, I know exactly what I wish to eat and order always, to everyone's amusement, a Veal Ragout considered to be a rather sophisticated adult dish. It tastes wonderful to me and is served on a real seashell. Sometimes there is a small band playing waltzes or melodious foxtrots while we wait for our meals to be served—I get up and dance on the dance floor. It does not matter that nobody else is dancing or that tiny tots usually do not do this, especially not in Germany.

Father is taking me, at age five, on a trip from Berlin to Holland. The car is parked in an underground garage with many others. Everyone has a private stall. It smells strongly of rubber and gasoline. An elderly man sits in a booth near the entrance, keeping an eye on who is going in and out and he will pump gas when needed, by hand, from a gasoline pump with a glass container on top. When he swivels the handle back and forth, the yellow fluid bubbles and somehow enters the car. Father has opened the hood of the car, and I point to a big sponge I see to show Mother who is on the balcony to watch our departure. That is when father closes the hood with my thumb in it.

The bleeding thumb was quickly bandaged, and we left with mother waving fond good-byes.

I enjoy the drive. I lie on the backseat with the hood open, looking up. The road is narrow and lined with trees on both sides, which meet at their tops over the road. Many are caulked white around their trunks. I assume that is for safety reasons I still do not know. They are heavy with green leaves, creating a roof over us. There is a slight *whoosh whoosh* each time we pass a tree. I am still looking for this kind of road.

We pass through Hameln, a German city with a folk legend. Father points out the carved wooden memorial: a young man with a saucy hat and soft leather boots is playing a flute, walking with thousands of rats following him, thus freeing the town of the plague.

9

My Father, whom I call Vati, and my Mother, whom I call Mutti—the German way to call your parents—are a very happy couple. Vati is six foot two, slender, with a generous mouth, a prominent straight nose, ears flat against his head where hair is sparsely distributed. I have seen evidence in the bathroom of some color adjustments to his hair.

His brother, who has sketched him, shows him to have long and wide cheeks. He wears dark-rimmed glasses over his sparkling small blue eyes.

Mutti is slim, blond, and blue-eyed with a lovely, friendly face, often taken for Emmy Göring, a movie actress and the wife of the pompous Generalfeldmarschall. She laughs readily, and I am used to hear her sing or even whistle a popular tune from a Strauss operetta or what is called a *Schlager* (hit) of the time. She dresses according to the fashion of the day, purchasing her clothes at Horn, an expensive shop with very good clothing.

A photo of her and Vati shows them in evening wear. They participate in diplomatic affairs and grand openings quite a bit. Vati is in tails and Mutti in a blue silken long gown. The evening gowns are ordered from a dressmaker who designs and then makes the dresses. I remember one made of dark purple velvet with a gold lining showing on the underside of sleeve caps.

We children have our clothes made by Frau Krüger, a slim middle-aged lady who comes to our house and sits all day at the sewing machine, turning out the most delightful dresses and coats. That machine is built into a table in such a way that it can be turned upside down, disappearing into the table when not in use. A metal pedal at floor level is activated with her foot to make the machine run. I love to watch the material slide along under the needle and the boxes of buttons and thread in all colors. I am anxiously watching Frau Krüger's finger getting too close to the needle going up and down in its sewing motion.

Scissors make a nice sound on the wooden table where the material is cut out. Mutti helps to open seams. Frau Krüger shows her how to do it carefully so not to damage the material to be released. Mutti is much too high-strung to do it that way. She uses a razor blade and then vents her distress when she cuts into the material. Micaela, my sister, and I are dressed alike. I still have the wooden buttons used on our tweed coats. Of course, we had to have light blue hand-smocked silk dresses for special occasions.

I still dislike to put on clothing today and I now realize that this has to do with what I had to wear as a child as underpinnings. Can you imagine a vest that covers my upper torso, a sort of undervest with at least five buttons to close? From it extend two long garters, two in the front on one side and two at the back, which keep dark beige ribbed cotton stockings up. Over that, in the winter woolen underpants, which covered the upper leg and were so scratchy. The stockings always wrinkled at the knees too. It was considered to be healthful to wear little boots to strengthen children's ankles. Mine were fine beige with patent leather, which had to be laced up. Slacks were only worn for sports, like skiing. Even ice-skating was performed in skirts; they were to billow when making turns.

10

Mutti tells me that singing is pleasant for a husband to hear because then he knows his wife is happy. He will, anytime he feels like it, grab hold of Mutti, who laughingly protests, but gladly gives in to his amorous enthusiasm.

Vati has a deep laugh; I hear it often. He owns a sports bicycle, yellow, with handles pointing downward and thick tires. He bicycled one time from Berlin all the way to Holland, I am told. It was something unheard of for an intellectual to do—no wonder his relatives consider him a bit wild. And who would ever wear short sleeved silky shirts—of color even?

He keeps a skiff on the lakes surrounding Berlin and I see him pull and stretch a spring exercise device. Well, he has to; he married a woman twenty-five years younger.

11

We always eat our main meals in the dining room at a large round table covered with a white tablecloth and linen napkins, the family silver and a vase with fresh flowers in the middle. Mutti had gone to household school in Berlin and prepares tasteful dishes, which, I later find out, are all from one little book, 138 pages, recipes covering many decent German everyday dishes and drinks, even suggestions on what to feed a sick person. I still treasure the booklet.

Whenever Mutti experiments, however, which she feels she needs to do to impress visitors, she gets into trouble. One time she makes a dish with peppers. It was not clear to her that they also come rather hot. That meal was not a success. Of course, children's observations are a danger. Mutti decides to prepare wild boar, a very pungent meat that has to be soaked in milk for a long time first. Well, when the time comes for me to do my curtsies to the guests at dinner, I mention, to show off how smart I was, "Mutti, is this the meat that smelled so terribly?"

We all get together for five food occasions, starting with breakfast in the dining room. We eat fresh hard rolls that have been delivered by a nearby bakery. A pink cotton bag with a drawstring is hung the night before on the outside doorknob. The rolls, baked freshly the next morning and still slightly warm, are placed in the bag. They are cut in half, with crumbs flying all over, and covered with butter and honey or a homemade jam. On Sundays, Vati gets a soft-boiled egg. It sits in an eggcup and is being decapitated with a sharp stab of the knife and eaten with a mother-of-pearl spoon. Silver spoons would oxidize. Tea is served, the real thing for the adults and malt coffee or linden blossom tea for the children. Then at 11:00 AM, it is time for a break. Hot chocolate is the favorite. One teaspoon of cacao with a teaspoon of sugar is stirred with just a few drops of water, and then the boiling milk is poured over that. I am allowed to do the stirring and I love to deliver Vati his cup in the workroom where he is busy writing.

Later, Mutti discovers health and we get a fruit salad with hazelnuts instead.

Lunch is really the main warm meal eaten, again, in the dining room. Then, in the afternoon after nap time, we sit on the balcony with tea and Dutch rusks, buttered and jammed. At 8:00 PM, a light supper is taken in the dining room, existing of breads, cold cuts and cheeses, sometimes with beer, a malt beer for me.

In the dining room, behind Vati's chair, a small Dutch clock stands on a special table. It needs to be wound daily with a tiny key, an impressive occurrence happening each day at dinnertime.

12

The time together at the dining table, especially at the evening meal, is the time Vati reports to Mutti the latest happenings around the world and especially in Germany. Mutti is listening intently to what Vati has to say. They glance at me and start to speak in another language. First, Dutch, because that is the language of our nationality but not what we mostly speak. Soon they realize that I begin to understand, and they switch to English. It is important that I should not hear what the parents have to discuss. In those days, conversation has mostly to do with the political changes in Germany. A child has the tendency to proclaim with great pride, "My father says . . .," which could be the end of my parents. The words concentration camp start to become a whispered threat. It was a new word—the understanding was of a prison or even a work camp, not knowing what was happening in Dachau and other places of horror.

Vati knows. He sends special secret reports to the Dutch government in The Hague about what is happening, also in the way of militarization. The reports are put aside because they do not fit into the Dutch commercial designs of the time. During the German occupation, the Gestapo discovers the reports in The Hague at the Dutch foreign office and come and raid our house in Berlin. Much later, after the war, the reports come to light and create a scandal. Even a film is made describing Vati's efforts, and a book is written in Dutch translated into German about Vati and these occurrences.

13

Illness is a big production in our household. My fever is high and the throat sore and a cough is wrecking me. Mutti has the antidotes. To bring the fever down, I am rolled in a wet sheet and then covered with a mountain of blankets. I am supposed to produce a sweat to bring down the fever. When the time has come to deliver me from this moist prison, I am rubbed with a fine-smelling alcohol called Franzbrandwein. I am exhausted and definitely do not like this procedure because I do not do what is expected.

Do you know that there are three ways to use a thermometer? Mutti insists on number three. This method is considered to be the most accurate where children are concerned, but three degrees are deducted.

Another drastic measure is the cough remedies. Linseed oil or even rendered fat is heated; I can still remember the smell of it. It is not that unpleasant, just peculiar. A wad of cotton is dipped in it and placed on my chest, fastened with a woolen wrap around me. I think Mutti first misunderstood the instruction; I remember having a chest with the linseeds themselves piled on me.

Mutti, under a standing lamp she brought, sits by me next to the bed, making me drink fennel tea to help with the bronchial congestion and linden blossom tea to bring the fever down and canned peaches to keep me going. A cool wet cloth is placed on my forehead. An aspirin is placed on a teaspoon and melted down with a few drops of water. Mutti looks very concerned, and I feel obliged to get over my illness. Even after getting better, I have to stay in bed another three days just in case. The floor of the room is washed with a Lysol solution to prevent the spread of whatever sickness is present. Ever smelled real Lysol?

14

Our doctor is Frau Dr. Gottschalk. She lives in our block, with an enamel nameplate on the door of her building, visible when walking by her apartment house. We like and respect and totally rely on her. She disappears out of our lives, with so many of our acquaintances and friends, who make up the pattern of our existence. I guess it happened after there is all that broken glass in the street one morning. The windows of some of the shops are smashed in and have lettering on them. It is so very scary. I do not understand. I notice that the park has changed too. The comfortable, inviting green wooden benches have a Star of David on them saying For Jews Only, but not all of them.

Also, some people have a yellow Star of David on their lapels saying "Jew." I do not understand but am not inclined to ask questions. There must be a good reason for it, and questions are not welcome. Vati brings the radio into the living room so that we can hear a speech of Adolf Hitler. It is not a speech, but a strange way of talking. Loud, with great pathos and long pauses, to give the audience the opportunity to endorse his statements with shouts of approval. I hear "Sieg Heil" and then the song "Die Fahne hoch" (Raise the flag high), the fighting song of the National Sozialisten. Vati and Mutti look at each other and say nothing; they do not look happy. I feel that this speech has some momentous meaning.

Somehow, life as I know it is changing. There is a veil of secrecy I do not understand. Comments and questions I ask are hushed without any explanations or answers.

15

I am six years old, and I do not feel well. I am in the bathroom. Dr. Gottschalk appears; there is much talk, and I am put on a stretcher and carried down the five flights of stairs and I then remember nothing. Then a white mask is put over my face, with an evil-smelling substance put on it drop by drop. I hear a strange humming and then nothing until I wake up with violent retching.

That hurts. My belly is bandaged, and in the days to come, once in a while, it is taken off, and white-clad nurses pull something out of my belly. That procedure is repeated three times: operation and belly treatment. I begin to lean over to one side to give more space to my insides. Everyone is so nice to me. I am in a modern hospital with large glass windows and am in a light large room. There is Schwester Erika always. One night I wake up, and I see her sitting on the chair. She suddenly disappears, and next, a large needle is inserted into me. I learn later that I had died. But I continue to live and get better. Two months in the hospital. Professor Seefeld was proud; peritonitis patients usually do not survive without the then-not-yet-discovered penicillin.

I get presents. Professor Seefeld gives me a Japanese garden on a platform—with a blossoming fruit tree and a Japanese lady under the tree, so beautifully real to life—and a doll made of felt about fifteen inches tall and dressed in colorful Biedermeier-period clothes. I treasure these gifts and take them home with me.

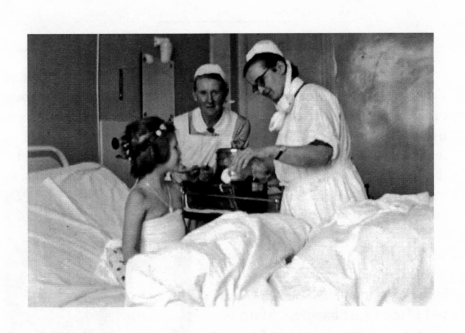

16

I have missed the start of the elementary school. There is a problem; Vati is *Doopsgezind*. *Doopsgezind* means that, when, as an adult, a choice can be made, fully understanding the meaning of the various religions. Being so very independent, his parents did not belong to a church, therefore Vati has to make up his mind, and *Doopsgezind* shows him the liberty of choice. That is out of the ordinary in the mostly Lutheran church climate in Germany. Vati has to prove that he is not Jewish.

Many letters go to Friesland in the Netherlands, our roots. Many a response is received, with proof of baptism back to the sixteen hundreds. Then Micaela and I have to get baptized. Mutti does her best. We are dressed in long lacy dresses. I have lost a few front teeth, which shows in my smile on the photo, and my sister is disgusted, it appears. But all goes well, and I am accepted at the elementary school.

The first day, I am sent off with an eighteen-inch-tall funnel with colorful pictures on it, full of candy; a leather satchel on my back, filled with a slate in a wooden frame; chalk and a sponge attached to the frame hanging out of the satchel. The school is a reddish stone building next to other buildings in the almond-tree-lined street. I walk to school. The teacher is Frau Frederking, a friendly plump lady with graying hair. I do well in school. Mutti never has to come to speak to the teacher. The mother of another student comes once in while, and we all do not think much of the student after that because the mother makes up to the teacher. A mistake. So there, parents who visit the teacher is a sure sign that something is not in order and is to be avoided. Mine never did.

Close to the school is a store with nothing but sweets, colorful Gummi bears—a fruity gelatin candy—and things. For a penny, a sweet can be purchased—not often because I had to ask for the money from Mutti. I did not get an allowance.

17

Mutti takes me to visit Aunt Minna and her husband, Uncle Max. We have to ride the S-Bahn and then a bus. Both work in the famous Berlin Virchow Hospital. They live in an orderly small apartment. They are hefty people without children. We are spoiled by Aunt Minna with soft-boiled eggs and other foods now becoming scarce. She will continue to be the reason for us to be alive when our existence during the war and after Vati's death becomes critical in every way. Tante Minna has all the strength and determination of her parents, my grandparents, the farmers.

I avoid my uncle, her husband, as much as possible. He has a way of pulling me on his lap that somehow makes me not want to be there.

This part of Berlin called Moabit is a working-class neighborhood. The apartment buildings all look the same: simple, gray, without trees and no elevators. The children of Uncle Max's brother taunt us when they see us pass by in the street. They are older, probably about thirteen years old, and they wear a uniform with a handsome brown leather knot to hold a black tie, part of the uniform of the Hitler Youth. This gives them status. They know that we are Dutch, which seems to give them the right to call us bad names. They scare me with their show of disdain, with their shouted remarks. Mutti pulls us along to quickly get away from them.

18

It is 1935 and a sister is born. A special nurse is present to look after her and Mutti. I look at her in her crib with lace and ribbons and think that she is beautiful. She, however, finds living difficult and lets the world know about it with continued wailing. Feeding her is a real struggle because she refuses to swallow. The nurse, Schwester Erika, tries everything in her arsenal of nursing tricks, even holding the baby's nose shut to make her swallow. Since she has advanced to spinach, the resulting explosion creates a problem for all. Nurse is dressed in a starched white uniform.

The doctors have no idea what is wrong for a long time, until a navel hernia is discovered and repaired. From then on, life is better for

Micaela. The name Micaela is chosen after deciding that if she is a boy, she would be called Michiel, a family name, and if she is a girl, Micaela is a natural.

Life with Mica, as I call her, is complicated for me. She is five years younger, and anything I do is being interfered with because she does not understand and approaches games or my toys as a baby does—of course, destructively.

19

There is music. Mutti sings her favorite operetta songs and "Parlez-moi d'amour"; there are records played on the Victrola wound up with a handle. When the handle needs to be turned again, the music plays slower and slower down to a whining sound.

Vati plays the violin. He decides that I have to play the violin too, especially since he finds a children's violin to add to his collection of string instruments. The bow is carefully waxed and the instrument is packed in a velour-lined violin case. That is where my interest for the violin ends. I have not the slightest feeling for the instrument and do not like the screeching sound next to my ear. Vati decides that I should try the piano. Herr Ventura is hired. His system is to teach his pupil to play from written music. I did not practice much; repeating the same piece over and over again made no sense to me. When sitting next to me, his pointer, with which he follows the notes I play on paper, has a tendency to slip and slide down the page.

We give up on the lessons, but I learn enough to play a piece right from the paper. When it has rhythm and melody, it goes really well too. When in music class at school where everyone had to play an instrument, I still hang on to play the piano although a recorder was played by many and could have been my way out.

I never attended a concert. When I reach that age, Vati has died and Mutti has to keep us going in a very tight household.

20

We vacation in Coxyde, a seaside resort in Belgium at the North Sea, an ocean with strong tides and a fine beach. I learn to ride a bicycle along the boulevard at the seaside, admire soldiers in fancy foreign uniforms and playing marches, and fish for shrimp, with a net designed for that activity. It is a wooden bar of about eight inches wide attached to a stick with a net. This is scraped across the sand in the shallow part of the ocean at the beach. The shrimp are tiny and transparent, and there are lots of them. They are a delicacy when cooked. Here I taste for the first time Belgian cooking, baked chicken with apricots. I am amazed; it is delicious and opens up a new outlook on food.

Vati comes from home to visit us for a few days. We eat strawberries on a terrace by the sea. I decline the whipped cream—it is too rich for my taste. Mutti mentions, "A time is coming when you will wish for it." Vati must have brought news, a forthcoming war. It is 1938. This is the last holiday I remember with Vati.

Mutti, Mica, and I traveled back to Berlin by train. We reserved a sleeper with shower. Wagons-Lits is the name on the side of the train. The compartment is lined with polished wood in inlaid designs, and the dining car with white linen tablecloths covering the tables, flowers in silver vases, and crystal lights. We eventually pass through Cologne. Mutti points out a cathedral, one of the finest examples of Gothic architecture. It is lit up and looks bright against the night sky. It is not very long before all the lights in Germany are dimmed.

21

Vati is invited to go to Poland; he returns deeply depressed. Mutti and I are walking in town, doing errands one day when I see a familiar face. "Is that not Mr. Horty?" I ask, remembering having seen him visiting Vati. Mutti signals me to be quiet, and we walk on in a faster tempo, not paying any further attention to him. Adolf Hitler is giving more speeches, sounding more insistent, more dramatic, glorifying the German people, pushing them on to more patriotic thinking. He feels that all German-speaking people should be together representing one glorious Germany, which he calls a Reich. So Austria becomes part of that Reich, and quickly, other military actions take place. Then suddenly in September of the year 1939, war was declared. Vati is taken prisoner but is treated as a diplomat and spends time in the Hotel Adlon, Berlin's poshest hotel, for three days. Then the Netherlands had fallen. There really had not been a declared war at all. German bombers, without warning, destroyed Rotterdam with everyone and everything in it.

22

I finished my four years of elementary school, and there are choices of schools, depending on what I wish to pursue in the future. My family, all intellectuals on my father's side, requires that I should go to a gymnasium. This is a school with Greek, Latin and all the sciences preparing for universities. Hitler does not allow this choice for girls. He believes that they must primarily make families. So Vati selects the lyceum in our area. It follows the curriculum of a gymnasium. A red-stone building where the letters *Königin* (Queen) *Louisenschule* could somehow not be obliterated by the Nazis. The stairs from floor to floor are made of dark gray granite, but the classrooms are bright with large windows. We have our own classroom, and the teachers come to visit us for the various courses.

I like the teachers. I realize now that they are trying to give us an education without the prescribed Nazi dogma. So there is Miss Buchin who is teaching us English but also "It's a Long Way to Tipperary," which we sing with verve, and we learn Shakespeare too. Frau Dr. Seidenschnur is adored by us all. We secretly call her "Strippchen". She makes us think, creating reasoning. This process has never left me; it is now seen as my arguing. She puts emphasis on Göthe and widens our horizon via large maps of the world on the wall, explaining topographical importance. Why do I remember the map of America so well?

There is Dr. Zedler who does have the Nazi Party button in his lapel. He also never spouts Nazi doctrine. Somehow, he suddenly is not there any longer. What had intrigued me was his experiment of throwing an object into a girl's lap. He was expecting that the automatic reaction would be that she would try to catch the object by stretching her skirt. Who knows? We did not stetch. Nobody talked about what had happened to him.

I have fun with art class and music. There is intense sport, considered a good thing for Aryan youth. One must be strong in body. Being blond and blue-eyed is a plus.

23

The first time I hear a siren announcing an imminent bombing raid, I get goose bumps and I shudder. The undulating sound is so penetratingly loud. There is no escape from what is coming; I feel a sense of helplessness. Why should this be happening? What have we done to be punished like this? A cellar area is declared as a place of shelter to go when the alarm sounds. It is obligatory. If missing, Mr. Hartung will make a report. The cellar is reached by about ten steps below street level, reached from inside the apartment building. Benches are placed along the wall. Along the ceiling, all pipes that supply water, hot and cold, are visible, and an escape hatch has been built up and out to the street. There is not much air circulation. At the beginning, the bomb attacks deliver mostly incendiary bombs and are executed by the British.

Vati stays in our apartment on the fifth floor, the top floor of the building. He is now bedridden with a kidney infection. The winter had been tough; Germany has no coal for heating the winter of 1940-41. Vati sits in blankets to do his writing. Dr. Obst visits daily and is frustrated, knowing about medication being developed against such illness in the United States and totally unobtainable.

Mutti is spoiling Vati with all the kindness and love she is capable of. To strengthen him, she prepares regularly a raw egg mixed with wine for him. I have a diary, like all the girls of my age. I do not write in it, but it is customary that your friends write in it a nice little poem or some kind words and add small colored pictures. I give it to Vati, and I receive it back with two pages in beautiful lettering saying "Du möchtest vom Vater ein kleines Gedicht, wohlan liebe Edith tue stets Deine Pflicht" (You are asking from your father a little poem—here it is: dear Edith, do your duty always).

One particular time, after the sirens are blaring and we are going to the cellar, I say farewell to my room; I look at everything, the last is my alarm clock, a Junghans Lautlos. I look around with the most peculiar feeling of foreboding. Vati stays in the apartment. He had had one look at the cellar and could not find any reason to look for shelter there. Sitting in the cellar with Mutti and Mica, the apartment building is hit. Vati, working his way down via the five flights of stairs since the elevator is not to be used during an attack, sees flames and throws the buckets with sand and water, placed outside each door in the hallway, on flames wherever he sees them—not a good thing for him to do because of his illness.

The apartment building is burning.

24

I do not remember what we did after that. I do remember going to school as usual and that I am wearing the same clothing for days. Something is happening to the school too. Classes are held in another building at an unusual time of day. I stand in the school courtyard and we have to sing the Nazi hymn with arms stretched into the Hitler salute *Heil Hitler*. That definitely hurts. There is nothing glorious to celebrate with song or any other way. Tears are streaming down my face, and I feel so confused and let down. I now experience this feeling over and over again when Haydn's melody, which Hitler had stolen to march to the death of a nation and a people, is being sung as a hymn at my church.

We are assigned an apartment of a German countess von Schreibershofen in the Flotowstrasze. I know right away that this is very different. The door to the apartment is made of a beautiful carved wood, opening into a hallway with bedrooms on the left and a bathroom on the right. Deeper into the apartment is a dining room, which leads through a door to the back of the apartment with the kitchen and rooms for the staff. Looking out over the Flotowstrasze are the bedrooms and a salon. The bathroom, dining room, and the kitchen area get their daylight from a courtyard. The building itself is four stories high, and the central staircase, wide and carpeted with Oriental runners. The stairs wind around the elevator shaft, a gilded affair. We are close to the Tiergarten, a park taking up part of the center of the old Berlin, the royal Berlin, with statues of generals and politicians of times gone by.

What a difference. Our own apartment had been built in 1929 in the art nouveau style. The outside was designated as Neubau, light gray, square, with large windows; the outside finish beige, full of little pieces of glass and pebbles; the street, broad, lined with linden trees. They smell so sweet in the spring. The building entrance hallway has marble floors; the walls, twelve inch green tiles with white spackle. A brass handrail gives support when climbing five marble steps to the landing with the elevator. The art nouveau style is followed through in the apartments themselves: the doors, the brass door handles, the pattern of the parquet floors. Mutti selected a china pattern by Rosenthal with an art nouveau design. I find the pattern again, much later, in a museum as typical of the times.

The wallpaper in the bedroom had an art nouveau pattern also, a light background with striped oblong forms.

Our temporary home is therefore a discovery. The chairs around the ten-foot dining table have high backs, higher than the person sitting on it. Each has a carved wooden crown on top. I find out that the crowns display five points, a sign of earldom. The salon has silk chairs and a bookcase filled with small leather-bound volumes of the *One Thousand and One Nights*. I lie on the floor and read them all. It takes my mind off the worries about what is happening to us, especially with Vati now bedridden. In the neighborhood street, I find a pile of sand and practice far jumping, again trying to block out the realities of our life.

25

Vati is getting worse and needs to be taken to the hospital. Mutti calls me, and I say good-bye to Vati before he is taken away on a stretcher. A feeling of utter helplessness overcomes me, and I cry bitterly.

While Mutti visits him in the hospital, he tries to communicate with her by writing into his calendar booklet. They are just long loops. An embolism is coursing through his body and ends up in his lungs and kills him.

I cradle Mutti. She is crying and is desolate. She is thirty-six years old with two children, ten and four years, her house destroyed, her husband gone. I had done my crying and saying good-bye to Vati, having the  terrible feeling that I would not see him again, that he would be gone forever. So to her astonishment, I console Mutti, "Vati does not have to suffer any longer."

To follow the German tradition, Mutti is dressed and veiled in black and will stay so for a year. I stay in the background, watching all the many people about. A service is given in the chapel belonging to the Queen Louise cemetery, and the grave is located next to that chapel.

I see photos someone has taken of the grave. It is covered with many flowery wreaths, their broad silk scarves showing who they are from. From then on, our Sundays always include a visit to the cemetery to tend to the grave, planting and watering and just sitting on the bench facing the grave with Mutti talking to Vati.

26

Mutti decides that the Dutch family needs to pay attention and maybe help us somehow. She has a portrait made of us three and decides that we need to go to the Netherlands to show our faces. We visit with Vati's sister, Tante Eeefje, and her husband, Oom Jan, who is secretary of the town of Arnhem. Tante Eef is a tender-looking woman with a narrow face and the small eyes of Vati. She suffers from migraines, and when an attack hits her, we have to  be very quiet. When she smiles, all feels well. Oom Jan is the friendly man with a white mustache. I enjoy the Dutch interior of their home, the grandfather clock with its deep, sonorous bell sound, the furniture passed on through the generations.

I learn how to make tea in the living room, with copper kettles, tea cozies and the seven minutes of soaking to make it just right. With it goes sugar and milk, and a cookie is always offered. Teacups are made of thin porcelain and the silver teaspoons are small and light. The typical Dutch breakfast I encounter consists of dense white bread with butter, and on it a choice of sugar mixed with cocoa or an anise confection and, of course, tea. In the middle of the morning, coffee is served with a cookie.

We also visit with a cousin in Naarden who has two boys. I do not feel that close to them. The family situation appears to be strained. Next we visit with the ex-mayor of Amsterdam by the last name of de Vlught, in his large home also in Naarden. His wife is a good friend of Mutti's from the good Berlin days. The interior of the home is impressive, with large windows looking out over an immaculate garden. The chairs in the living room have covers that are the needlepoint work by Mutti's friend. She is very kind to us and is somehow able to find shoes for me. They are very adult looking and pinch a bit.

Mutti is not used to not having a man to look after her. While at the de Vlught home, she takes a walk with us in a deserted lane and somehow begins a conversation with a strange man. There was nobody else in sight, and I am very concerned.

27

Mutti begins to call me Vati. When I start to talk to her with "Mutti," she immediately answers with "Ja, Vati," an awful responsibility for a twelve-year-old.

The Dutch Consul in Berlin, Mr. Millenaar, is now part of the Swedish Embassy who takes over the interests of Dutch citizens. The Dutch have no diplomatic representation in Germany. Although they were never at war, they are considered to be defeated by the Germans, who have taken Rotterdam by bombing it even though the country was neutral. Mr. Millenaar is standing by and helps us where he can. Mutti needs much help. She is like the women of her times, totally relying on her husband and never asking any questions. There is no life insurance although Mutti tries to cover this mishap up by suggesting that there must be something, probably in Switzerland.

We are seeing our own apartment for the first time after the bombing. Vati's room does not exist any longer; it was totally burned. The rest of the rooms with everything in them have been cooked and smoked by the heat from the apartments below. The flat roof allowed the incendiary bombs to penetrate the roof and our floors, turning the apartment below into flames.

The smell takes one's breath away. The furniture is blistered, and each item in the house is smoked. Mutti's linens, so prettily folded with a pink ribbon and carefully placed into her cupboard, have brown edges. Everything is brown.

We are one of the first buildings to be hit. It is still a sensation. The Germans decide to repair the damage, and we move back into our smoky house. Money is now a problem, and Mutti decides to rent out Vati's room and the maid's room with usage of the guest bathroom. A special telephone is installed, with a device that locks the phone until money has been placed into a tray and then moved sideways so that the coin falls inside the phone and activates the dial tone. Mutti enforces the rules she has given everyone, and it is actually nice to have two students move in.

Mutti is clever with things. For Christmas, she finds an old two-room dollhouse and some wallpaper, which we paper in the late evening when Micaela is asleep. Mutti has made a paste of flour to attach the wallpaper to the walls of the dollhouse and so is restoring it. "Do not tell anyone that I am using flour to make paste," she warns me. The dollhouse has a new look for Christmas for Micaela.

There are now food stamps. Because we are foreigners, our food stamps are blue instead of pink. People frown at us when they see them when we are shopping.

28

Before, when Vati was alive, Christmas was a fun affair when we are all together. I do not remember Vati ever being part of it, but I do remember the Christmas man coming, the German kind.

Aunt Minna, Mutti's sister, was there; the Christmas tree was adorned with balls and lametta, lit with white, real white candles, and gifts under it. Lametta are the thin aluminum strands hung from the tree branches. We have to sing before we are allowed to get the presents. Often there is much laughter because the Christmas man had imbibed just a tad too much. I recognize my uncle Max under the Christmas man getup, but do not want to disappoint the grown-ups.

Mutti does not have much sense of the mechanics of toys. I receive a beautiful doll. I tried to make it sit, and the leg breaks in half with a snap and the stuffing is coming out. It does not have a joint. How shameful for me to have broken my toy. I am crestfallen.

The Christmas after the fire, with Vati gone and the money scarce, is toned down. Just greens with decorations, but definitely cookies. There is a special cookie made in Nürnberg, spicy, covered with chocolate and baked on a wafer. There are anise balls rolled in powdered sugar and Stollen a sugary, buttery yeast bread baked with raisins soaked in rum and nuts. We also have Speculaas, a traditional Dutch cookie pressed into the shape of windmill, spiced with cinnamon and especially cardamom, covered with almonds. Mixed nuts with nutcrackers are in bowls and mandarins for the taking.

We also follow the Dutch tradition. December 5 shoes are set outside the bedroom door, and nuts and oranges are found in the morning placed there by Saint Nicholas, the bishop last residing in Spain who gives gifts to children on his birthday. In fact, in Holland itself, he arrives on a white stallion, dressed as a bishop, with his Moorish helper in his Arab dress, turban, and all. They arrive officially on a boat in Amsterdam. Black Piet, the Moor, carries a sack with gifts but also a switch to punish the disobedient children. No, they do not come through the chimney, and there are no reindeer.

In homes, a game is played involving everyone. Fun poems hidden in various places, with hints on where to find the next one are read, often making fun of the recipient, who finally finds his gift, only to discover that it is so tightly wrapped that it is difficult to unpack. Sinterklaas may open the door and throw nuts into the room. The Sinterklaas tradition has its roots in the eighty-year war between the Netherlands and Spain. In Holland, Christmas was actually strictly a religious celebration for a long time. Gifts were not given. We are in the country of Calvin in the north and the south is mostly Catholic.

29

I am back in my own school with my friends. The bombings begin to become very dangerous and threatening to our lives now. Different bombs, different airplanes, louder explosions, several attacks during one night. We are taught to cross our arms over our chests and open our mouths when hearing the howling of a bomb nearby, this to prevent our lungs from bursting. We are tired, sometimes sleeping only three hours a night. School goes on. The walk to school goes along destroyed buildings, still burning. How many bodies are buried under the rubble? Broken gas lines exude their typical smell mixed with the stench of rotting human flesh. The lake in the park is covered with green netting trying to change the topography of the city to confuse the bombers. I have to go on; in my mind, I have to hold on to everything I have learned and am used to. Life as I know, it must come again. This is so terrible, unbelievable, so I have to be strong. I have to survive. There is no choice.

In 1943, Mutti says, "When Göbbels himself recommends that all women and children should leave Berlin expecting heavy bombings, it must be getting very bad." We move to a small village west of Berlin where

Mutti's sister, Tante Frieda, and her husband, Onkel Heinrich, live with their daughter, Trutchen, my cousin about five years older than I.

We rent a room in a house without plumbing of any kind. We bring a sofa from home that sleeps three comfortably. I hate the place and try to make it more beautiful by waxing the floor with shoe polish. Mutti is not happy. Now the floor is smelly and slippery too. Washing under the pump outside and the outhouse are part of our existence. It is hard to stay clean. All that is normal and dear to me lies behind me, but also burns inside me.

We see the bombings on Berlin and the resulting red fire glow in the distance, the bombers coming over our part of the country from the west. They enter the ring of the defense system, brilliant in the sky found by spotlights then the flashes of the antiaircraft guns. When a plane is in real trouble, they let go of their bombs to be able to reach higher altitudes. That is then happening in our area. Now we have no hiding place, not even just an unlikely place like the cellar under the apartment building in Berlin. A plane is shot down; it comes closer and closer, lower and lower. We cover our ears and cling to each other. It crashes into a field, a walking distance from where we live. Mutti does not allow us to go and see but returns telling us that a little dog found the scalp of a man. It was concluded that he must have been a Negro.

30

In its heyday, the village was known for its production of a fine liqueur. The Gilka family distilled, bottled and sold it. They were the owners and lived in a French-style chateau in a park with a driveway ending at a wide staircase. The iron gate was impressively designed. Large wooden doors open to a vestibule with more doors leading into the main hall. A high and wide fireplace to the right and French doors look out into the terrace behind the chateau and the beautiful garden. To the right, a wooden staircase winds itself expansively around a pillar to the floor above. A dining room and library and many other rooms are there also, but I have forgotten.

The Gilka family also ran a farm estate with horses to ride and hunt, and cows, pigs and other farm animals. The buildings housing the animals and the equipment to tend to the woods and fields form a large square, all important enough to employ an administrator and a farm manager living in homes attached and part of the estate. The village has a school, a church, some small farms, and one village street.

I need to go to school. Potsdam is the nearest place with a lyceum. To get there, a bike ride is necessary to make it to the adjacent village where a scheduled bus rides to Potsdam.

Vati's yellow sport bike is brought out of Berlin for me to ride to school.

We go and see what is happening in our apartment. We bring out of it what we can carry. The Dutch family silver, a Delft shaving dish, and one by one a three-hundred-year-old Dutch cupboard, which can be taken apart.

We have boarders in the apartment. There is a very elegant Belgian lady, slim, pretty, with the most coquettish hats I have ever seen, which she makes herself with feathers and veils. She and others are part of some sort of a workforce brought to Germany.

The trains do not ride directly into and out of Berlin any longer. The rails have been destroyed, and the ride goes via any line that is still functioning. It takes so long.

The Gilkas are long gone, and young military families live now in the chateau. Feeling sorry for us, they invite us to take some rooms on the third floor, formerly used as rooms for the maids and other staff. What a relief—running water! The children, Horst and Ina and I ride to school together, first on our bikes and then the bus to Potsdam. We enjoy each other, and the bombings are concentrating on Berlin, so the trip is relatively safe. School is difficult because the courses are different, but I do my best. A lovely girl in my class does not show up any longer. I hear much later that her father, a German nobleman and high-ranking officer, together with other men of the same background as von Stauffenberg, tried to kill Hitler. This is not publicized much in the radio news, the only source for news at that time. It is July 20, 1943.

The rumor in the village is that flying ace Ernst Udet is coming to live in the chateau. Also General Kurt Zeitzler, the man of Stalingrad. But neither one arrives. They have been killed by the Nazis, it is rumored.

31

We eat at my aunt's. The kitchen has the dining table in it, and I watch her activities. She has a stove for cooking that needs wood for fuel and has iron rings of different sizes she skillfully removes with an iron tong to make the pots fit. All cooking seems to start with bacon, the slabs hanging in the pantry. Her chicken soup is delicious, with vegetables, noodles and potatoes. We seem to have that often. The favorite cake that is always on hand is Streuselkuchen, a flat yeast cake with butter crumbs on it. Tante Frieda makes her own cheese, waiting for the then-unpasteurized milk to turn sour, which also thickens it. Then the milk water in a piece of linen is pressed out. This mass then is boiled with caraway seeds added. The cheese is aged by leaving it in a cool place and is ready to eat when turned transparently yellow. It is sharp and unacceptably smelly but very delicious especially on the German grain-seed bread. There is a bread soup and a soup made of brown roasted whole wheat—food I have never eaten before. A true adventure. We also eat stewed lung—a sweet-and-sour preparation—and boiled tongue with a wine sauce and many wild mushrooms, but I am used to these dishes.

I help my aunt in her garden. It is a piece of land walking distance from her house but not attached to it.

All sorts of vegetables grow there. I am intrigued by the process of putting a tiny seed into the earth and then, when the time has come, to pull at the green above the earth and, surprise, a perfect carrot appears. Asparagus is hidden in long mounds a foot high. The earth cracks a bit.

That is the sign to dig up a white spear of asparagus. Vines produce cucumbers in abundance. Potato and tomato plants have a strong smell I like. I am still searching for that smell, which then, in a lesser degree, moves on into the tomato with the warmth of the sun still on it. There are bushes with berries, the sour red grapes of the red currants, and the furry green balls of the gooseberries. I am picking them for Tanta Frieda into a basket hanging from my arm, for her to make jellies and jam and, once in a while, a fruitcake. I eat them too while working. Too much temptation.

It is decided that I need some other activity to keep me busy. With a horsewhip in my hand, I go from farm building to farm building to take their geese to the meadows surrounding the village. The animals are gray in color with yellow beaks. The geese scare me. They are big and have a bad temper. When they are really mad, they stretch their necks, spread their wings, and with a hissing sound, come running toward me. My horsewhip is my only defense. While in the meadows, I am also to pick greens for the rabbits. Still, today, I know which weed to cultivate in my garden here to avoid the rabbits from nibbling on my flowers.

32

The radio, the only source of news in my aunt's house, is being listened to with attention. I remember Vati's map in the guest bathroom on which he followed the Russian war with a pen. At this home, we have to follow the war in our minds seeing the map of Europe. I am nervously listening. The news is not that positive any longer; although the activities are negative at the German front, the news still tries to make all positive, with plans of action that will glorify the German cause.

The Allied planes discharge strips of aluminum to confuse the German radar, I learn later. They make a whistling sound descending to earth.

We children gather them and weave them together for decorations. Leaflets with terrible pictures of German atrocities, also dropped by the Allied planes, frighten us. I see one of them and, if I remember correctly, they must have been pictures of tortures in German concentration camps. We do not understand. No way would anybody do such terrible things to another human being. We are told they are American propaganda and to not pay any attention to them.

I was shot at by a fighter plane when bicycling back to Kartzow. I was able to jump into a dugout along the road.

I hear a plane fly over, making a different sound. I can distinguish American plane engines from British planes, but this is totally different. I look up to see where the plane is in the sky but cannot spot it. This happens a few times and then I suddenly discover that the plane is way ahead of its sound. A German plane. Amazing. In this confused time, not having a father to clarify the upcoming questions, I keep quiet. Nobody mentions it. I know now that this was the first jet plane ever.

Now the time has come when we listened carefully to the news. The German front, although retreating, is still hailed as being in good shape and not to worry about a thing—Germany cannot be defeated, it is too strong, thanks to the strength of the German people. This kind of news stays on, deep into the last days of Germany. The reality is, however, frightening. I see Ina and Horst and their families driven away in a German Army truck. My heart is sinking and I feel that what lies ahead is darkly threatening.

We pay attention to where the Allied troops are and where the Russians are. Then we hear for the first time cannons to the west. That must be the Americans, and we breathe a sigh of relief. But then, no more advance. The cannon sounds quiet down, and there is nothing. The question comes up: should we walk to the west where the Americans are? Considering the practical aspects of food, money, and lodging is a painful process. What to do? This is the worst part of this time of the war. As civilians, we know absolutely nothing. All communications are down. Mutti chooses to stay with her sister and her husband, her family, providing some support, she hopes.

I must escape the reality of the looming danger. I take a walk into the far end of the castle garden and discover five giant fir trees growing in a circle; their branches reach the ground forming a chamber. I push the branches aside and enter; the stillness, the pungent smell of the trees envelop me, and the softness of the pine-needle carpet make me lie down and look up into the height of the trees. The stems, so old and strong, give me the feeling of security and the continuation of time. This is my temple; I feel the strength of nature, possibly God. I go here often.

Looking beyond this part of the park, I find bushes with purple elderberries hanging in ample fullness from their branches. I gorge myself with their sweetness, wondering about their generous gifts to me.

I am standing outside. There is an eerie stillness. The noise of the engines of hundreds of bombers in the sky making the earth vibrate, the howling and then the explosions of their giant bombs—that has curiously stopped. The cannons in the west are not heard any longer. The radio broadcasts, our only source of information at this time, have stopped. I feel a bottomless, cold emptiness inside me.

Behind the wall of some buildings, a few children are standing around. They know me. I suggest we play a children's game, something sweet and happy. And that is what we do, holding hands and singing. It is as if the world has stopped. I do not want to think. I want this moment to go on forever.

33

Then the sound of heavy trucks. We look and see American-style trucks, but they are the Russian army. Soldiers on foot are behind them. They look very foreign, and they no longer have boots on, only rags around their feet. They have marched continuously from Frankfurt/Oder around Berlin, creating a wide circle around the city. Soldiers with rifles are knocking on our doors looking for German troops. There are none; there never were any. The soldiers are like something out of a play, so foreign and macho, with tight belts around their waists and expressions of hatred on their faces. We have the paper with the Swedish flag and a big stamp on it, which, when shown, seems to help. Not that the soldiers know how to read, I think, but the stamp does its work, and they leave, letting us alone.

Then on the road that leads along the village, German Red Cross trucks appear and drive on to the west. Then people with carts and their few belongings follow.

There is no end in sight of this pilgrimage. They are evacuating Berlin, hoping to make it to the halted Allied front at the river Elbe. However, Russian fighter planes suddenly appear and methodically shoot the whole trek. The Red Cross sign makes no difference to them. When all is stopped and killed, they fly on. The road is piled high with corpses. The men of the village decide that they have to bury as many dead as possible. Wounded are carried into the castle. There is no medical help, and their screams are heard through the night.

A few people from as far as East Prussia—Königsberg—are alive and find shelter in the castle. They have made it to our village and no further.

Mutti has our suitcases in a cellar to try to protect just a few of our things. We discover that we have been robbed. All our jewelry is gone. Still, today, I look for the beautiful things I received from my Dutch relatives at my baptism. It hurts deeply. Are we not all in the same boat at this time?

We go back to the castle where we had made our home in the servants' quarters with things we had been able to rescue from the bombings in Berlin. We could not enter our rooms. They had been trashed and used as toilets. I feel brave, go behind the castle, and find that the valuables stored in a great room by the families who lived there are strewn all over the lawn. I rescue some small leather-bound books by Schiller. It just is not right to leave them there. For whom? There are bloodied hand-embroidered linens, just lying on the ground, forgotten. Mutti gets hold of some of them. We see our civilization trampled into the dirt.

34

We huddle in Tanta Frieda's house, sleeping there too. Russian soldiers are coming through the house, probably not looking for German troops any longer, but for what they consider to be treasures, watches mostly—and women. I am now fifteen and need to be hidden from the brutal raping of women that is going on. I sit at the table in the kitchen, making myself small by shrinking as deeply as possible into a chair between a wall and the table. I still have long hair in stresses, which, when braided close to my face, make me look much younger, I hope.

One day, new trucks roll into the village. A knock on the door, and it is explained that Tante Frieda's living room, which has a door to the outside, is claimed and outfitted as a dispensary because the chateau is now a hospital. The pharmacist, also a high-ranking officer, introduces himself with a wide smile of gold teeth. He is from Uzbekistan, he tells us, and has Mongolian features with the fuzzy black hair typical for them. We are somewhat relieved because this means protection from roaming soldiers, although we are not familiar with Mongolian habits. The pharmacist likes to socialize. He comes into the kitchen and offers us vodka and sausages and enjoys our company, not knowing much German, but smiling broadly. The vodka is drunk out of a full water glass in one hand, and a smoked fat sausage held in the other. He tries to communicate and proudly tells us about his son. He has a pharmacy, he tells us, and wishes to buy me from my mother as a wife for his son. We are concerned.

Not long after that, the pharmacy and the hospital are closing down, and their employees leave.

Again, the uncertainty of our existence—what comes next? More Russian troops, this time regular white soldiers, are occupying the area. The raping is starting up again. I look out of a back window of Tante Frieda's bathroom; I have the stairs of the castle in view in the distance. There is a melee of two or three people; then a shot rings out. The daughter of the schoolmaster has been killed, refusing the advances of a soldier.

There is a high-ranking officer part of the troops who tries to keep order. We carefully venture out again. The Russians are now working the farm part of the chateau.

Walking through the village, I hear happy music coming from the local café. The Russians are playing their instruments and singing. That is so remarkable that I am drawn to the happy sound. The soldiers are dancing, and suddenly, a young fellow grabs me and we are dancing! The whole occurrence is unbelievable, a hole in the world of horror. It was a realization that this person, too, was away from his home and his normal life—a moment of understanding and joy, each of us dancing wildly a Russian folk dance.

35

Mutti is not feeling well. A truck arrives, and she is loaded on the truck bed. Tante Frieda's house gets a one-foot-wide white stripe painted around it—the international sign of quarantine. Cholera is ransacking the population. We are not allowed out of the house, nor is anyone allowed in. We have no idea where Mutti was taken nor whether she is still alive. Some relatives are trying to find their kin by walking to the nearest hospitals. Some are raped and killed. All we can do is wait. As soon as the quarantine is lifted, we hear that Mutti is in Potsdam, in a hospital. Of course, there is no food, no care there. So I decide to take food to Mutti. A backpack is prepared with foodstuffs. I try to disguise myself, putting on leather shoes much too big for me, old nonconforming clothes, do the thing again with my hair and shuffle off to Potsdam. This means that I have to defend myself to the death if accosted. I arrive at the hospital. Mutti is unapproachable because of the cholera. I sit awhile on a stoop and acquaint myself with the situation. When the right moment arrives with nobody around, I run into Mutti's room and hide the food under her blanket, then run out as fast as I can. I have no idea of the distance from the village where we live to Potsdam; remember, this distance when going to school was covered by bicycle and then by bus. I do this once a week, round-trip in a day. This put something in my life that never left me: the resolve not to die, the hatred of the thought of what could happen to me. Much later, when connected with Johns Hopkins University in Baltimore, Dr. Livingstone was researching whether once this steeliness has been tapped, would it ever go back to normal? He thought not; once the rubber band has been stretched to its utmost, it will never return to its resting form, he concluded. I know.

Life in the village takes on a sort of normalcy under the occupation of the Russian troops who have taken over the running of the estate, something not easily done because they do not speak German, and of course, there are many misunderstandings. The trick is to get food. Working for the Russians at the farm is one way of getting grain, this as payment for working at the farm. Mutti survived, is back, and gets the job of shearing sheep. For years she had the impression of an angry sheep's hoof on her leg.

36

It had been decided that I should return to Berlin, not to our house, but to the apartment of Hilde and her mother.

Hilde—well, how long do I know her? It seems forever. She was in the same class in the Volksschhule when we started at age six, and slipped with me into the lyceum. We hung out together and had great fun together, enjoying the same activities. We ran much, especially up the stairs in our respective apartments with which we had trouble because we found everything so funny that we doubled up with laughter. A definite handicap, we tried to beat the elevator.

Hilde had a friendly family, Tante Elfriede and Onkel Walter. They visited often. They were seated around the dining table in the afternoon, for the traditional coffee and cakes with the rest of the family. They were pleasant, and they seemed to enjoy themselves with a lighthearted way of talking. Hilde's mother was somewhat fragile and more reserved. Hilde's grandmother was usually seated near their balcony door with a view of the park and its lake. She knitted much, and Hilde had the prettiest outfits. One was a red skirt with a multicolored attached vest, which I especially admired.

And then back to the lyceum. Our school building was still standing and we had the same teachers.

Hilde had a clear intelligence. I was so grateful for her helping me with algebra—a hopeless undertaking for me because I tried to approach algebra with mystical reasoning.

The day after the war ended, Hilde's father was shot and killed by a Russian soldier. A professor at a boy's college, he had decided to go and have a look at the college.

To survive, we ate weeds and boiled acorns for protein. Mutti supplied grains in which worms had started their lives, but cooked; after the first-time gagging, we ate all.

We attended school again. Charlottenburg. This area of Berlin was under the British occupation. We felt fortunate. The city felt safe, and we walked to our school without fear. I do not remember where I slept in Hilde's apartment, only that her grandmother had died and there were no services for funerals. She definitely stayed too long with us.

Later in 1946, when I had left Berlin and was in boarding school in the Netherlands, Mutti and Hilde and her mother stayed close. That was good to know. Hilde was totally reliable.

On my visit from the States to Mutti and Micaela in Berlin in 1985, I visited Hilde, who by now had become a nurse at a religious order. She was dressed in a starched white uniform. The Johannesstift. Later, Hilde started to travel, and we visited with each other in Washington. Then she married Mr. Schulze, who unfortunately did not live for long. I did not understand, but shortly after Hilde married, her mother hanged herself. Now Hilde and I talk on the telephone. She still feels close to my family, calling my sister once in a while. Two years ago, when traveling in Europe extensively, I included a visit with Hilde. She looked at my travel plans and decided we should meet in Stuttgart. That would mean midway between my Amsterdam to Bad Salzuflen train trip. All I had to do was to get off my train and stay a few hours with her in Stuttgart and board later in the day to go on to Bad Salzuflen. She was coming from the north of Germany to meet me. Well, wouldn't you know, she had arrived a few hours earlier and had arranged a sightseeing trip and then some time in a Konditorei where we took up the thread and comfortably enjoyed each other's company just as when we were back in the old days. This kind of warm togetherness can only be enjoyed when one has been through a rough time together. For this kind of togetherness, I am very grateful.

37

Mutti and Micaela left the village and the aunt and uncle, and we moved back into our home, the apartment in Berlin. It had survived the fighting, except a grenade from a Russian tank had hit the children's room and produced a gaping hole. We closed all the doors to that room, and since central heat was of course not functioning since  nothing was functioning, Mutti obtained an iron stove. The pipe led through a window where the glass had been removed and replaced by a metal plate to let the pipe go through. Where to find fuel? We found out that the famous Grunewald, a forest by the lakes near Berlin, was providing wood. But you had to cut down your own tree and bring it home. I have no idea where Mutti got the tools and the cart, but off we went walking, probably at least seven miles to get to the woods. The tree was sawed and felled and sawed into pieces again. Yes, Mutti and I did that and then we loaded the cart and wheeled it back. We had wood, and at night, the featherbeds and hot-water bottles kept us warm. Mutti went back to the village where Aunt Frieda was supplying us with vegetables and eggs. Since asparagus was a luxury, we sold it at a high price just knocking on doors of our city-dweller neighbors, who were very grateful. The black market was the only source of edible and inedible things. Mutti was able to exchange a beautiful Persian rug for a pound of butter. We existed from one day to the next. People were desperate, living in and on a pile of rubble and nothing to eat. I went to school and noticed women in the streets picking up stone rubble and trying to put it aside in some kind of order. Life in the streets was dangerous. We children were told to walk in groups and not to use the underpasses.

One of my schoolmates disappeared.

The word was that human flesh was sold on the black market.

38

Vati's son, Hein, and his family had come back to the Netherlands after he and his family had been incarcerated in the Dutch East Indies by the Japanese. He had been forced to work on the infamous Burma railroad, later made known by the movie A Bridge on the River Kwai. He contacted Mutti and offered to make arrangements for me to come to the Netherlands. It is 1945, and I am fifteen years old. The decision was difficult for us. But it meant help for Mutti and a possible future for me in my homeland. There was no public transportation. The Dutch consul, Mr. Millenaar, again pulled strings.

I remember a difficult farewell from Mutti and Micaela. I stepped into a Red Cross ambulance with a few others. We were told not to talk and be totally still when reaching the Russian border outside Berlin since this transport of civilians was, of course, illegal to the Russians. At the last moment, a child not much older than two years was pressed into my arms. When the time came about an hour and a half later, at the Russian border, we were dead silent; our lives depended on it. Suddenly, the child began to cry. I had to hold its mouth shut. We made it through. When I arrived in the Netherlands, I was dropped off at the house of Vati's friends near Hengelo. They owned a resort called the "Waarbeek." They were the friends who had helped to smuggle Jewish artworks out of Berlin to the Netherlands. I knew them; it was an extensive family, everyone working at the different aspect of the place. Mutti, Micaela and I had visited there in 1941 after Vati had died, and we needed to be in touch with the family. I was making myself useful then; it was summer and I sold ice cream from a small white booth. Now I helped out by polishing all their brass objects, and there were many. I was taught that once the polish is removed, one has to continue rubbing until no more black is found on the polishing cloth. Dutch homes treasure their many brass objects. They are large and are mostly found around the fireplace, buckets for wood and kettles on stands to boil water for tea.

I read the Pearl Buck books I found on the bookshelves in the warm and comfortable living room. Nobody ever was in that room, and I made it my temporary home. After Berlin, this felt like a peaceful heaven. I had no idea what would come next. One day, Mrs. Smit excitedly said that I should have told her that I was supposed to move on to Hein. He was waiting for me to arrive.

39

The next step I remember is being delivered to a boarding school in Hilversum. Miss van den Oever and Miss de Coque were the directresses, with various other teachers. A school was attached, and two houses were occupied with living rooms and bedrooms for the young ladies.

I was stunned to be accosted by a beautiful dark-haired girl who spat into my face calling me a fascist murderer. She was Jewish, and my strong German accent provoked her.

I fell ill with a high temperature; the doctor was called who concluded that I had a reaction to the recent experiences of the war. I stayed in bed for a month and then did not speak. Miss van den Oever, a specialist on how to handle damaged souls, moved me into the main house into my own room. She started to work with me, escorting me to the post office to buy stamps, going to stores to buy shoes and a beautiful dress I was allowed to select myself, eating ice cream in an elegant restaurant. Slowly, I accepted that there was still normalcy somewhere in the world, and I was becoming part of it. There was control over life here. My accent stayed with me all through my life. A handicap, making it clear that I was not really from where I happened to be.

Where school was concerned, I had made it in Berlin to the class one year before the finals the Abitur. I first entered and then finished the school attached to the boarding school and received my diploma from it. Miss van den Oever felt I was ready to go to the local HBS, the Dutch equivalent of the Berlin lyceum, just for the last class. The directress of the HBS turned that down; I think she was snubbing Miss van den Oever—a bit of competition between the two ladies. It was decided I should go to a private school in Amsterdam—a bike ride to the Hilversum station, a half-hour train ride to Amsterdam, and then a tram to the de la Raisse Street. I was in good company in a small room at the back of one of Amsterda typical homes. The program was self-study under the leadership of a professor. I tried but the system did not work for me and we gave up. I was tired and mentally not ready for intense and disciplined learning.

Life at the boarding school became very pleasant. I felt protected and cared for. We learned to speak French and English in our daily activities. Each table at mealtimes had a different lady who spoke her language, which we had to follow. A young outside acquaintance of the directress was a designer, and I modeled his clothes. It was fun to know him and his beautiful French wife. We danced ballet together, just for the fun of it.

40

It was decided that I should have a job. In Bussum, a half-hour bike ride from Hilversum, a job was available and I was accepted. I was drawing electric circuits for the Rochester Sign and Railway Company, who tried to sell their product of American rail signals to the European market. The office was bright, located in a handsome villa. I worked with four other people in two rooms and a boss in his own room. I had not the slightest idea why what I drew did what it did. The explanations by my coworkers were not good enough, made no sense to me. I struggled along.

One could take a break in an adjacent small garden. I sat at the pond or rested in the grass and enjoyed the splashing of the water, looking up watching the clouds float by.

41

I still do not understand how deeply I was destroyed, how unusual my life had been. I know it now. Mentioning this is not as an excuse, but a realization.

Here I was in the company of regular persons, working with them day by day. I felt for the first time since my father's demise, the nearness of men. A new experience, their casualness, their sense of humor. After the closeness of the directress of the all-girl boarding school, this was a new step, new borders to be explored. The persons I came in touch with had no idea of my history and the desperation it had created. A man fell for my outgoing neediness. He, unfortunately, left a family and his children for me.

How young I was and how naïve. We lived an incredibly simple life; the husband gave up his job and found another at the Shell Oil Company whose headquarters was in The Hague. As soon as a divorce was realized, we moved to Scheveningen, the resort of The Hague on the Atlantic. We lived in one room in a villa until an apartment became available. For lunch, I remember eating one herring with a piece of bread. My inventiveness helped us through the meager times. Meager they stayed because he had to upkeep his young family. With the equivalent of a PhD from Delft, he had a good position.

I spent my time at the beach behind the high dunes and taking lessons from the Dutch professional tennis champion. The courts were behind where we lived. We slept in one single bed, and I complained about pains. It was decided that I had a cyst, which needed to be removed. This happened in the hospital of a scientist who believed in the power of color. A cheerful place. All went well. I felt that a new life was, after all, a possibility.

We got married in a civil ceremony I do not remember. There was nobody but us. Mutti could not come, of course, but wished us happiness by letter.

I started to experience me and the life around me. We now lived in an apartment in a respected neighborhood. It had just been built, and I enjoyed the large windows letting in the sun, making the place look cheerful. Those windows with their proximity to the sea had to be washed every week because of salt deposits. There was money now to buy a gray English tweed suit for me at a rather posh store in town. It had a plissé skirt. The jacket was too traditional for my taste, and I had it altered to give it the French cut, rather tight at the middle. Next to the store where I bought the suit was a fashionable shoe store, so shoes were bought as well, fine leather pumps with a two-inch heel. I always wore high heels; every lady did. My friend from boarding school, Ingeborg and I had long discussions about what made a perfect shoe, and that seams on the matching handbags were not allowed. I still have the wooden lasts that came with the shoes with the store's name on it.

Somehow, I was the owner of an old sewing machine, a Singer. It looked like a small suitcase made of wood. One took the hood off and placed the bottom on a table. It worked beautifully. I turned its handle and sewed light green long curtains to cover the windows of the apartment for at nighttime. Nobody in the Netherlands covered the windows with anything in the daytime.

When a party at the Shell Oil headquarters was announced, I sewed myself a fancy mouse gray dress and made a little matching hat. I used a hot pink ribbon around the décolleté and on the little hat. It helped to have rather good figure. I think I looked stunning.

42

Not long after that, my husband announced that he had been promoted. He was put in charge of all the refineries in Indonesia as process-control engineer. This meant our moving to Sumatra where we were to live in a camp because of political reasons. We started to follow the offered course to learn to live in the jungle and to learn the language. Because I had lived with the daughters of plantation owners, now disowned, in the boarding school, I had heard many stories of their lives—the servants and their mysticism, the proximity of tigers and snakes, and the hot tropical climate. Learning about our future was therefore not that foreign to me and held some excitement. We were, however, appalled when we heard that the Indonesians had removed the snake serum from the camp. This not only meant that our lives would be in danger, but it made it quite clear to us that the Indonesians were still carrying a deep hatred toward the Dutch. This was not good. Both of us had just survived a war. We were just starting our lives, working hard toward a peaceful, good future. Living in the Netherlands was not that exciting either; it was a socialist country with a large involvement of the government, which meant when something was needed, a request in the form of the necessary paperwork had to be sent to the government, and after a long time, one got an answer—hopefully positive. There was not much drive; all went along slowly. We wanted more; we were full of energy.

Friends suggested we look in the newspaper and we did. There was an advertisement by Westinghouse in the United States. They were looking for engineers. We got in touch with them, and an appointment in London, England, for an interview was arranged. In those days, one went by sea, crossing by steamer overnight from the "Hook" to Harwich. I will never forget this trip. The sea was incredibly rough.

In London we were booked at the Mandeville Hotel, very British, with lots of flowered wallpaper and plushy chairs. I experienced my first English tea—strong as coffee, with milk. Very flavorful. It became one of those good things making life pleasurable from then on.

We had been accepted, and the trip to the United States was in the planning. The trip was paid for by Westinghouse, and so was the move of the furniture of which we really only owned, a handsome wall unit. To obtain a visa to enter the States was a major undertaking. Fortunately, we lived in The Hague, where all countries had their embassies since it was the seat of the Dutch government. We tried to learn about the United States and especially about Baltimore, our future home. We found two pages on Baltimore in a booklet, with a picture of the Washington Monument on Charles Street.

43

The *New Amsterdam*, the largest ship of Holland America Line, was to take us over the Atlantic. It was 36,000 tons, a sizable vessel for its time. It would take seven days of travel. We felt that we needed to spoil ourselves and travel in first class, looking forward to a large cabin and the fine restaurant. It is October 1955. Up on the covered promenade deck, deck chairs could be hired, and we did that. Next to me, Professor Boak had his chair booked. The ship surprised me with its displayed artworks, the thick carpets, and the ample staircase. We sailed and said good-bye to Europe, our birthplace, with a lump in our throat. This was a major move into an unknown future and an unknown continent.

The ship, regardless of its size, started to move more than anticipated.

The sea was losing its calm and flat surface. The sky looked ominous. I had to hold on to handrails walking along. I did not enjoy the meals any longer and was told that it was best to be out in the air on the promenade deck in my deck chair. A thick woolen blanket kept me warm. The ocean decided to rise and fall in huge mountains of water, the crest of the waves sometimes as high as eye level. The wind was loud. I started to live in my deck chair. At one time, on my way to my cabin, I stood at the top of the wide staircase looking down when I was lifted up and placed at the bottom without taking a step. Dr. Boak told me that he had a heart problem, and it had been suggested he should go by ship instead of flying. The ship trembled after smashing with a thud into the next wave. The large windows on the main deck forward had been pushed in. At one point, looking aft, I saw a huge wall of water looming way higher than the ship—a rogue wave. I held my breath. The power of it all. Somehow, we were not swallowed up. But I will never forget that moment. We were thrown about like a cork.

It appeared that we were in a hurricane, and the ship could not move much. But we finally reached New York, although two days later than scheduled.

The buildings looked old and run-down; we had docked at Hoboken. Our papers were checked, and we had to wait for our luggage. It was rather late in the evening. It was dark when we finally stood in New York. We hailed a taxi and asked to be taken to the train station to go to Baltimore. We were certainly not prepared to be spoken to in Italian. The driver must have understood us though, and we made it into a train. It was an old type of train with worn-out leather seats. To my delight, a Negro with a white jacket and a cap smilingly supplied us with clean white pillows. It took many hours to arrive in Baltimore; the train made many stops, but we finally, rather tired, arrived in Baltimore at Camden Station. Three taxis stood in front of the station, but no one was paying any attention to our arrival. It was very quiet, nobody around. We walked up to a taxi and made ourselves known, but he did not move—dead, we anxiously assumed. The next taxi took us.

44

Westinghouse had made reservations for us at the Lord Baltimore Hotel for the next two weeks. The hotel was located in the heart of town, close to department stores, shoe stores, and specialty shops selling elegant bed linens and things fancy.

A young man from Westinghouse picked us up with his car to look for housing for us. My heart sank when I saw what he thought where we should be living. I had other ideas. I remember driving through an area of villas and seeing an apartment building. These apartments had just been built and were in what was called Guilford and Roland Park. This was more like it. We rented a one-bedroom apartment. It had a large living room with dining extension, a large bedroom, bath, and kitchen. It was also air-conditioned. Here it was October, and the clothing I had available were heavy tweeds and woolen pullovers, the sort of thing one wears in October where we came from.

We needed a car to get my husband to Westinghouse. York Road had several car dealerships, and I took a fancy to an Oldsmobile. But reason prevailed, and we decided on a new light green Plymouth. I think it cost $8,000. The Oldsmobile would have cost $12,000, too much.

A driving school was called, and I was picked up at the hotel and learned how to drive in downtown Baltimore. I still drive like a taxi driver when in the busy center of a town. Once when I drove through the intersection of Lexington and Howard Street, I was stopped by a rotund policeman. "You entered the intersection on yellow," he said. "But officer,

I just came to this country," I tried. "Well, you are not going to be here for long if you do not obey the rules." He smiled and sent me on. Still, today, I stop at a yellow traffic light, keeping an eye though on the mirror, to make sure I am not being rammed by someone not remembering the rule. I drove my husband the eight miles to Westinghouse at the airport in the morning, and picked him up in the later afternoon. I liked driving.

Some furniture needed to be bought. I do not remember how I found the stores. I think we had to be very careful again with money. This store was around the corner from Howard Street, going west. I bought a pink modern sofa. The salesman was extremely friendly; he seemed happy even. I also found a chair, an imitation of the Baughman-design chair, very modern too and comfortable. The cocktail table had been made before, to my specification, in the form of a Y in metal with round ball feet and a glass top. This, together with the wall unit we had brought from Holland, all looked rather good together. For a dining table, we had decided on a black metal table with cushioned chairs. It became clear later that this metal furniture was used as garden furniture.

We met a nice couple and invited them over. They declined the cake I had baked. I found an excuse to go to the kitchen and fell into my husband arms. What a disaster. But I kept my cool. This must be an American thing, I thought with a sinking heart. In Germany, you see, the cake your hostess has baked, you eat it and you give compliments. This was not my only experience. Another couple, this time for dinner, I thought they expected something typically German, and I made Kohl Rouladen, the recipe I found in my mother's cookbook. In her household, this was considered an exotic Polish dish. Later I found out that the Polish immigrants had brought this dish with them to the States, and it had turned into an ordinary American meal known as stuffed cabbage.

There was no holding me back. The next dish was tongue in a wine sauce. I served this to a colleague of my husband's and his wife. He excused himself after a short time, and I heard what I thought were retching noises.

45

So here I was in the apartment of my liking. There were really no people around to make friends with, and I felt that I needed to get into action. An interview with the department of labor in town was interesting. My dexterity was tested. I had to place blocks of all shapes into the holes of the matching shapes. That was completed rapidly. The interviewer had doubts about my working in a factory, and what about the five languages I spoke? "I know the librarian at Johns Hopkins, how about my making an appointment for you?" she suggested. The interview there must have gone well. I was added full-time to the staff of the history and geography department of the Johns Hopkins University to help Miss Lough, a certified librarian. I made 55¢ per hour. The library was located in the most historical building, creating a U shape with buildings on each side facing a wide lawn, all built in colonial architecture, with a white tower holding a bell on top of the library building. Inside, the professor's offices looked out over the front lawn. The history library on the second floor was located toward the back, around a shaft providing daylight. It smelled of old books and was very warm, no air moved; large standing fans provided some relief. Students who needed their books for their courses approached a desk, supplied the number of the book, and I then had to go into the stacks, which were off-limits to anybody else, and find the book, which then had to be stamped with a due date. I did not understand a word the students, with their various accents, were saying. Now what? There were racks with small drawers in them, containing the records of the books the library had, with their title, author, and where they were to be found in the stacks. Each student from now on had to supply me with that information by writing on a little piece of paper I supplied to get the material they needed. It worked to my great relief. I was so happy when I found the item asked for in the high stacks full of dusty books, no complaints, and Miss Lough went along with it too. She was a prim and good-looking lady, with a small sweet smile, and very helpful, but one knew to do as asked right away.

Oh God, the man who in the hallway once opened his raincoat scared me half to death. What a sad thing.

The cafeteria was the place where I and my colleagues had lunch. A fun group of young people. I learned from them about all sorts of things. They talked about what happened in their lives and gave their opinions on what was going on outside of it. This was part of my education into American life. I was warned that the mayor was part of the Mafia, which meant one was careful about criticizing the running of town.

46

We realized that we were too isolated in our Charles Street apartment and started to look for something suitable. People we met and liked lived in the north of Baltimore, and there we found a place: ground floor apartment, living/dining room, and two bedrooms, with a nice kitchen and bath. I sewed curtains, and we liked it. A good move, we made friends with couples living there. A bus took me to work. I tried to plant marigolds but did not realize that they needed earth better than what surrounded the apartment. They did not look good. Going shopping was easier too in that part of town. I could walk to a shopping mall, not very large and at that time not covered. I found an item, other than food, I just had to have. They were three canisters, yellow plastic, with gold tops in different sizes, and lettering in gold indicating what they were to be used for: sugar, flour and coffee. Plastic was new and came in many good-looking designs, an extravagance because we were very careful with our finances. I discovered Robert Hall on York Road selling inexpensive clothing. I could always make adjustments, but I fit a size 12 just fine.

Food shopping was done in an A&P not far from us. That was a surprise. In 1955, nothing was imported. All the food was grown or produced in the States. I was looking for lettuce, asked where I could find it, and was steered toward a display case filled with what looked like cabbages. No imported cheeses, nothing Italian, no frozen food. This I had to get used to—again, an exciting challenge.

Everything was to be learned: how people communicate, other than language, attitude, humor, polite exchanges, customs, behavior.

In order to find our equilibrium, we drove Sundays to Washington and spent the day in the National Museum of Art. We felt at home amongst the art. There was always an interesting lecture highlighting a special exhibit. A quartet played a concert near the fountain and a restaurant offered food. I still am in awe when entering the museum. Somehow, this is how the Romans in their glory days must have felt, I think. The entrance hall with their huge green marble pillars, the white marble hallways with their sculptures, and daylight shining in through the ceilings—this was good.

On Saturdays, we explored Baltimore. We found ethnic neighborhoods, each with their own styles of houses, shops offering their typical goods advertised in their own language, and their churches. We discovered the rows of houses with their scrubbed white marble steps Baltimore was known for. These were Polish, Russian, and German parts of town, shiny and neat as a pin.

In the northern part where the villas were, I ventured into structures under construction, not quite completed, to find out what the interiors looked like. A learning experience.

The time had come to purchase a television set, black-and-white, and a record player. We were fascinated by Jackie Gleason, who had a fine way of playing a tune on his trumpet with his own orchestra as backdrop. That was also the period of excellent family-oriented television shows of which there are still reruns shown today.

47

Somehow, life slowly lost some of its glamour. After almost a year at Westinghouse, my husband had not been able to obtain the required security clearance. This meant that he could not be part as yet of the core of work he had been hired for. There was little verbal exchange between us, and my husband was sullen.

I was unhappy and felt deserted.

It was decided that I should go to Europe, visit my boarding-school friend, Ingeborg in the Netherlands, and my mother and sister in Berlin. I obtained a leave of absence from the Johns Hopkins library, a steamship reservation in tourist class was booked, and I left. This crossing was calm, and I enjoyed the company of my fellow travelers. This was entertaining.

I have a photo of my winning a prize in a contest designing a crazy hat. After arrival, I was picked up in Rotterdam by Ingeborg's husband and in his silver Mercedes Benz sports car we were off to Leerdam where Niels Burgers, the husband, owned a successful international lumber business and lived in the house of his father, a roomy house with a flower garden and tennis court. It was grand. In the afternoon,

ON BOARD R.M.S. NIEUW AMSTERDAM
Holland-America Line

blankets were spread on the grass, and as a snack, yogurt was served with Dutch rusks. We were observed by two or three cats, the birds were singing, flowers spread their sweet aroma, and one could hear the small stream running peacefully by the property.

Ingeborg and I decided to go to Amsterdam to look at the elegant shops and to enjoy coffee with a sweet. She also introduced me to a handsome tall acquaintance of hers who, to my surprise, immediately took a shine to me. Wow, this was something new. He took over and insisted that I stay, and he showed me Amsterdam. He was  twenty-three years old, and I, twenty-five. He was getting his degree in economics from the University of Amsterdam, and he insisted that I just had to be his lady during all the planned festivities.

There was a horse show in the Ascot style. Dress up was required in the British tradition. I spent a whole night designing and sewing the necessary clothing and dressing a fancy hat for the occasion. Hans introduced me proudly to his friends and generally spoiled me in a grand  way. The horses and their riders performed well, and champagne was generously offered to the viewers. The ball turned out to be quite elegant, held at the Lido, one of Amsterdam's finest restaurants along a canal. A band played our kind of music, and we danced, becoming oblivious to the rest of the world. I am afraid we fell in love. How wonderful this kind of feeling I had never experienced, and how terrible.

48

To visit my mother and sister in Berlin, I took the train from Amsterdam in the morning, arriving in Berlin in the late afternoon. This train showed on the side of each wagon with metal signs where the train was going and the stops it would make. The final destination was Moscow. Berlin was still an island within the Russian zone. The city itself was divided into the Russian zone behind the impenetrable "wall," the British zone and the French zone. The part of Germany as a country in which Berlin was located was occupied by the Russians and ruled by them. The after-war made it necessary for them to build a barrier between the east and the west. The east was everything occupied by the Russians—Poland, Estonia, Lithuania, and Germany—and was run by them with suspicion and iron control. I hid all my reading material and tried not to look too interested in the landscape we traveled through. Their agents passed by in the corridor to keep an eye on the passengers. Some were in uniform and some in black leather jackets. Readily recognizable. They had boarded the train just before the border. My American passport was taken, and fortunately, there was nothing inside to raise their suspicion of the purpose of my travels, and again returned. This now was no-man's-land. Nobody could have helped me should they have decided that they would take me off the train and arrest me for some trumped-up charge.

Then we rode through the border, a high fence with a half kilometer of carefully raked sand behind it and outlook posts with soldiers and their drawn rifles.

The apartment of my childhood, with its grenade hole, had been repaired, and Mutti and my sister were delighted to see me step out of the train to take me home. Things had changed. The trams had disappeared, but the park was there again. I enjoyed Mutti's cooking. She was surprised that I mostly asked for the everyday dishes: Harzer Käse, a sharp Bavarian cheese, and the various delicious German sausages. We enjoyed the balcony as of old and had much to talk about over the traditional coffee time. Mutti was not happy about Hans. In her mind, I had done well marrying an established gentleman and making it all the way to America, away from the still suffering Europe. And then what did Hans, a student, have to offer? Hans came to visit, however, and together with the young children of the Dutch consul, we traveled as diplomats in a diplomat's car through the "wall" to see the other side of Berlin. Well, we were young and did not realize the danger we put ourselves in.

There was some kind of market, and I saw for the first time sophisticated Russian women in uniform but beautifully made up. We were interested in Russian records. The Russian choirs are wonderful, and I bought one. We communicated in  French, which I later learned was the language of the upper class in Russia.

Hans returned to the Netherlands, and I listened to all the reasons why I had to return to the States from Mutti and her friends. My heart was breaking; here was something I had to do again. Hans returned to Holland.

I tried to put this dilemma out of my mind by meeting with acquaintances of my sister who felt that they needed to entertain me. I ended up riding in the back of a motorbike and riding in a boat on the Wannsee. The last acquaintance did not behave. At his house after the boat had been secured, he entertained me and tried to rape me. Well, fortunately, without damage to me. But I was shaken. It took me until a few years ago to understand that men are not after your mind and your kind intentions. Did I mention before that the president of the office where I had worked had tried the same thing? I had been so honored to have been invited to his house, thinking that his wife would be there. Growing up without a father or brother, in the very unusual circumstances as the war, knowledge of the masculine mind-set was totally missing. I was and stayed very naïve.

49

The time had come, as had been decided by all but me, for me to return to my husband in the United States. I saw Hans in Amsterdam at the train station. He did not at all like my stories about motorcycles and boats. I sailed across the Atlantic to the States. My husband was glad to see me. He noticed my reserve, however, and began to ask questions.

I finally broke down; I simply had to tell him about Hans. He kept on pressuring me. He deserved to know the truth. After all, I had come back to him. He, however, was furious to the point of slapping me. That was not allowed. When he had gone to work the next day, I packed a suitcase and pulled the door shut behind me. I am not sure where I went, but I ended up in a furnished apartment on North Calvert Street close to the Johns Hopkins University. The job at the library was gone. I had stayed away too long for the job to be kept open. I made an appointment and was accepted as a secretary with Pan American World Airways on the corner of Charles and Fayette streets. That was a break because I had no money whatsoever. I remembered the dedication of the Dutch consul in Berlin and got in touch with the Dutch consul in Baltimore. He was active as consul mostly to clear ships arriving at the harbor. But he patiently listened to my story and kindly lends me $100.

Pan American needed to train me, and I was sent to New York to headquarters. I stayed at the Barbizon Hotel for Women, a hotel for single ladies, and attended the classes dutifully. Bob Myers had a way to instill enthusiastic salesmanship into his pupils, which I never forgot. The training took three months, and I took it in New York City. The word was out that a television channel was looking for contestants for their show *The $64000 Question* I think it was called. I applied and was accepted. We were trained by giving us lists of questions and their answers to remember. I was dropped because I said that this might be a good place to mention Pan Am. Later the program was in deep trouble because the training that took place beforehand drew attention. The show

was cancelled, but the expression "That is a sixty-four-thousand-dollar question" lingers on in today's language.

A girl at the hotel invited me along to an outing on Long Island where her lawyer boyfriend had a summer residence. I was lonely and went along. Again this was not good. The boys expected the ladies to entertain them. I was spared, fortunately, because these men were powerful and dangerous.

I passed the Pan Am end exam and came back to Baltimore to my job. A Pan Am uniform was ordered, and I fit right in. Everybody was nice and had a good sense of humor. However, my typing was not a success, being slightly dyslexic, which, I realized much later, resulted in my having to repeat the letters over and over again. We used typewriters in those days, threading the original with the needed copies into the roll of the typewriter with carbon paper in between. A typing error resulted in carefully erasing the original and the copies. A tedious activity.

It became clear that my typing time was over. I was placed in the sales department out front facing the public, behind a counter with a world map behind me on the wall showing the routes the various planes were taking. It was just up my alley. My various languages came in to play and my knowledge of Europe. I will not forget the "around the world" project. I pointed to all the places Pan Am was flying, easily found on the wall map. The breaking point for the airfare was Rangoon, with all the stops one wanted to make going either eastbound or westbound. Dips into the Southern Hemisphere became more complicated. The suggestion was then to do an around-the-Pacific trip, flying from the west coast via  the South Pacific islands. Australia, New Zealand, Hong Kong, and back to the west coast and then home. We made hotel and tour reservations. No computers; it was all done by Teletype. This was part of the job too:

appearing on television shows and presenting awards with the governor of Maryland. It was wonderful, and I felt successful.

Our boss, a lusty man, announced with great satisfaction that we had reached the one-million-dollar sales figure. I was proud.

50

My first encounter with God was when I sat at the scrubbed wooden table across from my grandfather at his farm in Pomerania. He was eating breakfast, a porridge made of oats. He cut a slice as big as a man's shoe sole off the home-baked bread and covered it with dark brown syrup from sugar beets as accompaniment to the porridge. No butter; butter was considered a spread of its own. Before starting a meal, he said a prayer, which I do not remember, but what did impress me was that we had to stop eating when a thunderstorm happened. "God is angry," he would say. He said very little, ever. I only saw him at mealtime. He was busy with his sons in the fields. I knew that he sang in the church, and when the highly respected minister visited, that was considered an occasion of importance. He looked at me with his blue eyes across the table and wiped his broad white mustache.

My aunts, who were busy around the house and tending to the small animals, did the cooking, baking of bread, and the drying and storing of fruits for the winter. Sundays, a sheet cake was baked, a typical dense German cake with Streusel on top. It tasted of butter and vanilla, delicious. Grandfather would dunk his piece in his coffee.

Everyone at the farm lived in the shadow of God's wrath or blessing. My aunt Frieda, the oldest, had a treasure of sayings that applied to any occasion, mostly predicting dire consequences of one's poor behavior.

Back in Berlin, I remember the church by the Lietzensee park, a simple building. We did not attend services; that was dangerous under

Hitler, who had his philosophy of the German Übermensch. Jesus did not belong. And besides, as foreigners, we had to watch our steps. The church had been spared from the bombs, however, and religious teachings were begun there right after the war's end, which I attended in order to be confirmed. There was again the realization that there was a power available, when Mutti, at moments of great danger, would exclaim with intensity, "Lieber Gott, steh uns bei." It was this realization that there must be this *Gott* who was protecting us. When the Russian troops arrived at the village where we had gone to elude the bombings, I was standing at the window upstairs in the little bedroom of my aunt's house where we lived, and prayed. I knew that He and I were not in close contact, but at that moment, He was needed. "God," and I was really concentrating now, "let me live, even if it is only," and here I was looking very far into the future, "until I am fifty-seven years old." He saw me through the raping and the killing, but when I reached the age of fifty-seven, I knew that I had to pay up. At the time, I was attending a course at church and finally admitted to what I had bargained for. "You cannot bargain with God," it was explained. I was very grateful.

I was still wearing my hair in braids because I was fifteen years old in 1945 and that was proper. A dark blue dress was found, adjusted, and a white color attached. The confirmation took place in a church I had never seen before. We were about twenty youngsters to be confirmed. After all the doctrines I had been exposed to, I had a reluctance to accept a new one, but because of my grandfather, I thought that this needed to be part of my life. I received a confirmation document with a text I had to select from the New Testament and became a confirmed member of the Lutheran Church. Mutti had lost the drive, Mica was too small, so I did not continue formal attendance of the services at our little church by the park.

Fifty years later, I received an invitation to attend the celebration of the first class to be confirmed after Hitler; I had been part of it. I was touched, had had no idea.

I did not go.

I thought that it might be nice to be part of a church community. To be part of the American life was paramount. The Methodist Church on the corner of Charles and Lake Avenue looked so cheerful and friendly, and I attended a service there. Lutheran looked as something I should try because of my German heritage, also the Presbyterian Church. None caught my imagination. It was not until I got married to Dick Foley in 1962 that I found my church home. He insisted that we attend every Sunday, even though we had to drive from the Towson area, twelve miles into downtown Baltimore to attend the services at Emmanuel Church. Dick felt that the discipline of attending regularly was important. Dr. Alfred Starrett, the priest, held sometimes controversial sermons. They fit into the times of social change and were supported by his ten years in China, which included much yin-and-yang philosophy. I warned him, "One of these days, someone is going to challenge your ideas." "I wish they would!" he answered. The beauty of the church softened any thought that seemed to be threatening our conservative outlook on life. The large choir added depth. They consisted of trained voices; the Peabody Institute of Music was just around the corner. Margaret Freed sang her solos way beyond the required level of a church service. Our heavenly gain. Dick knew about singing since his voice had been trained by the Peabody and Mr. Bibb as well, although he did not pursue a singing career. After the service, we gathered for refreshments and conversation in a special room with comfortable furniture and a library.

Then I was confirmed by the bishop and became active in the Altar Guild, an exclusive group I later understood. We met regularly for an evening meal after which the church was put in order. Water was boiled in big kettles to soften the wax clinging to the candleholders. The linens were washed, ironed, and put back with pink ribbons into their designated drawers. And the church had to be dusted. That included the altar, even the benches, and this was a large church.

In Bethlehem this Holy Night,
Was born the Son of Endless Light.

He came to us with no demands:
A helpless Child with empty hands.

He brought one gift we all can share:
His endless Love; His will to Care.

A. B. S.

Christmas Greetings

and

Best Wishes

for

the New Year

from
The Reverend and Mrs. Alfred B. Starratt,
The Reverend R. Douglas Pitt,
and
The Vestry of Emmanuel Episcopal Church

The Chancel of Emmanuel Church
at Christmastide
Cathedral and Read Streets
Baltimore, Maryland

I realize that I was drawn to the colorful formalities. Behind the altar, carvings reached high up, covering the entire wall. There were two chapels on either side. From where we usually sat, on the right side, we had a view of a life-size white marble angel holding a basin. This was the baptism chapel. Sun coming through the stained glass window behind it gave the statue a special shiny glow. On the other side, that chapel was rich in wooden carvings, reminding me of the fancy works found in the churches in Bavaria or Austria. I felt at home.

Dick and I were not allowed to get married in the Episcopal Church because both of us had been divorced. Friends introduced us to the Second Presbyterian Church in Guilford, and Dr. Warren was willing to perform the ceremony. First, of course, seated across from his desk in the rectory, we had the usual session of pointing out the importance of the sanctity of matrimony. On October 20, 1962, the church wedding was held in a small wooden chapel on the edge of the Chesapeake Bay on Gibson Island.

51

Dick and I met in May on board the *Lord Baltimore* at a Chesapeake Bay excursion with dinner and dance organized for the travel industry. We saw each other across the room, and I was immediately intrigued. Here was a person with the same family background and thinking, I found out later when we dated. And he was quite handsome in a distinguished way.

But before that, there had been Geza. Five years . . .

After returning from Europe, I worked as librarian at the aeronautics department at John Hopkins. The word was that a Hungarian student was in the hospital with an appendectomy. I went to visit, and he was pleased to see me. He had been part of the Hungarian Revolution and suddenly saw himself in another country, another culture without a soul he knew. We bonded.

He stood by me when I had medical problems in a most generous and comforting way. His mother sent colorful Hungarian handcrafts, rugs, pillows, and a pair of beautifully embroidered slippers. When I moved to an apartment on Roland Avenue, he even built a bookcase for me. All of this still surrounds me. I was deeply involved with him for five years. We had being European in common and each other, but our backgrounds did not mesh. He was angry; it was hard for him to adjust.

Dick Foley fit so well into my life and into my thinking. I felt that I needed to abandon the Hungarian student, although with a sinking heart.

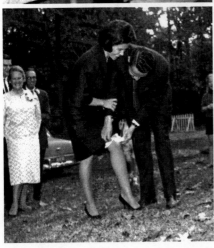

Dick and I decided to get married on October 20. Dr. Warren agreed to the location: the little chapel by the sea on Gibson Island. The island is small with a house here and there, a yacht harbor, and you have to pass a gate to get in.

Mutti and Micaela had come from Europe, and Dick's family was there. Alex Dietrich was the best man. Zsiga Toth gave me away and really scared me when he whispered, entering the church, that Dick had fainted. To my great relief, there he was in his full handsome glory, and the marriage then executed lasted for twenty-three exciting years until death parted us. A reception in the house of the Wolfe family, friends of Cindy Sturgiss, a friend from work, followed. These were intimate, warm moments.

Dick was slightly taken aback when he was to release the garter then to be thrown on to the onlookers. But he managed after a slight hesitation. Photos were taken. I kept all the proofs.

Our honeymoon was a preview of the life to come. Dick had committed himself to an experiment he believed in, bringing cruise liners to ports other than New York harbor. His reputation hinged on the success of filling the berths

of a ship sailing from Baltimore. Moore-McCormack with their *Argentina* participated. This was so new an idea, and the convenience was remarkable. Persons from Pennsylvania, Virginia, Washington DC, and beyond liked the idea of leaving their cars on the port territory and their drive was certainly much shorter than to New York. Dick himself, then working for American Express in Baltimore, had booked seventy persons. Well, this became our honeymoon party. Photos were taken by the press, and we made it as a headliner into the *Baltimore Sun* newspaper.

We had rented the ground floor of a large house on Orkney Road. It had a bit of a garden in the rear. Our motley collection of furniture had to do. In fact, we never bought new furniture ever. I still have a chest of drawers in my living room, which we bought secondhand for $5.

52

The mail waiting for us included a call to the courthouse for my citizen procedures the day after our return. First was an office interview. I was not prepared for the question: "Under what name do you want to become a citizen?" I had no idea. Was there not a law one had to follow? The clerk was waiting for an answer. "Excuse me," I said, standing up and running to the top of the large marble stairs at which bottom the relatives of the applicants were waiting. "Dick," I yelled, "what is my name?" He was nonplussed but then understood my dilemma, and he solved my problem. First, the first name, then the maiden name, then the legal last name, and that is how I became Edith Noordewier Foley in the good American tradition. The ceremony in the courtroom hall was deeply impressive. I was reminded of the duties and obligations to the United States of America, of the cut of any previous associations with any other nation or birthplace, the possibility to carry arms against such nation or birthplace. In those days, dual citizenship was impossible.

I had to wait at least five years before being considered for my American citizenship. The year was 1962. These were the immigration laws at the time: quotas were assigned to countries from which persons were considered to enter the United States if needed. I had entered in 1955 with my Dutch husband because Westinghouse needed engineers, which granted me alien status and a green card.

53

Dick worked for American Express on Charles Street, selling travels and organizing conventions to groups. I worked for Pan American World Airways, the American flag carrier. Pan Am had Juan Tripp as founder and president, who was said would wander the street to look into the offices of the company just checking. It was an exciting time. Once or twice I was even stationed at the airport to check in international passengers for their flight. In the city office, I sold airline tickets, of course, but also tours, booked hotels, and made sure that health regulations were followed and visas obtained. We had fine reference material; the customers never fared wrong.

What annoyed me were businessmen coming in just to chat. They were "coming on to us." What an embarrassing nuisance. "And they are married," I thought. Many years later, John Gray, PhD, published his research in book form titled *Men are from Mars and Women are from Venus*, a charming explanation of men's and also women's behavior. It then all became very clear to me.

54

Dick was obviously doing very well in his job. New York headquarters of American Express noticed and promoted him to a position at the Wall Street executive office. It was a difficult decision to make for him. Dick sat all night in our little garden, thinking it over. He decided in favor, one had to move on in life and one's career. It was decided that I would drive to New York and look for a place to live.

A new highway had just been opened connecting Washington with New York City. The ride was smooth on the six lanes winding through a wonderful landscape. No billboards on either side anywhere. There was also no traffic. It seemed as if I was one of the few cars on it. Today we know it as Route 95 and avoid it when possible because of its congestion.

"We absolutely must not live in Manhattan," Dick decided. "Too busy, no moment of quiet." Long Island became, therefore, our choice. A pleasant real estate agent showed me around. It turned out that she was the mother of Gordon McRae, a then well-known performer. I remember his happy singing in the show *Oklahoma*.

After several roundtrips to New York City and beyond, a small house was found fitting not our taste, but our budget. After the Second World War with the soldiers returning, housing was scarce. A Mr. Levitt designed and built a whole village of small affordable homes with a bit of garden near Westbury. It became known as Levittown. We were right in it, 9

Plum Lane. This was the first time I entered a house with the kitchen right by the front door. We moved. It was 1963.

To reach our respective offices, we drove to the Westbury railroad station to take the Long Island railroad to the edge of Manhattan, where we changed to subways. Mine to Forty-second Street and Dick's to Wall Street. Total time traveled one-way—one and a half hours. Mr. Waterhouse, the manager of the Pan Am office in Baltimore, pulled strings, and I was ladled into a plum job, working at the street office at Rockefeller Plaza. From the Forty-second Street subway station, when reaching street level, I had to brace myself against the unending compact stream of people heading toward me. And the wind was so strong and terribly cold in the winter.

The Pan Am ticket office was very fancy, the showplace of Pan American World Airways, still the flag carrier of the United States. A modern eight-sided skyscraper proudly proclaimed their importance; the Pan Am Building in the middle of Park Avenue, crossing it. This is where I saw in one of the hallways Mr. Charles Lindberg, who, together with Juan Tripp, decided where their planes should fly, thus establishing the world routes for the carrier. It was said that a woolen thread was held on a globe connecting New York with Tokyo, and this was the way these men established the polar route.

Here are a few of the occurrences at the office where I worked. Daily, a fancy elderly lady arrived at the office, opened up a small black leather satchel, pulled out a little spray bottle and some tissues, and cleaned all the phones. I thought that this must have been a Russian princess who had fled the communist government, arriving in the United States without income. Juan Tripp gave her this job. I liked that idea. I still do.

We stood on rubber mats behind a long counter, probably five or six agents at one time. A small round wooden disk could be pulled out to sit on. But we did not; we needed to reach the computers we had to use in front of each of us. Ah, the computers, so new. In fact, we were the first office to try them out. The management did not take chances. Psychologists were standing by to help us through any kind of crisis.

Across the counter were seating arrangements for about twenty persons, always crowded with people who needed our help changing their plans or getting information. This required organization. One of us was designated to be the "floor walker" for an hour or two per day, directing the next in line to the proper counter position.

The floor was a fancy light-colored stone or marble. Anyway, my feet, in their high heels, suffered. They spread into one size larger and needed the help of a podiatrist. But it was an exciting time in our office in the heart of the city, helping people from all over the world.

Did Dick and I enjoy Manhattan? No, we were there only to work. On weekends, we were too tired to think about anything but relaxing at home. The people we met maybe lived in New Jersey, three hours away from our home. But we had careers and made money.

55

Dick was contacted by Guy Erway from Baltimore. He owned the WAYE radio station the first good music station in the United States, an insurance agency, and a travel agency in Baltimore. He was planning to sell all and thought that Dick might be interested in the travel agency.

We visited Guy Erway and his family in his house in Baltimore. He explained that he was moving to Florida and getting rid of his businesses. All he owned were well run and first-class operations. The travel agency, located at Sutton Place, was called WAYE Travel. The radio station was located in a penthouse, and the name in large letters visible for blocks away proclaimed its existence there. The travel agency on street level had been designed and furnished by Chambers, a well-known design company. At the entry, as a reception area, stood two chairs and a small table. Today I still own these chairs, although reupholstered, and the table. They had cost $500 each in 1962, quite pricey and rather classy. The color scheme of the walls and furniture was light blue, with yellow built-in cupboards and large sturdy desks. We needed $10,000, the purchase price of the agency. Dr. Zsiga Toth, seeing an investment possibility, lent us this amount, and we purchased the agency. What an excitement! American Express New York did not want Dick to leave, telling him about their plans for him as a vice president. In those days, it was considered good business sense to place management two years here and then two years somewhere else, not necessarily places of one's choice. Dick was a Maryland man and was glad to be able to return to his home state.

We rented a townhouse located at the former Ruxton rail station, easily reached in twelve minutes from downtown by Route 83 heading straight north, leaving the city behind. Ruxton is a neighborhood with individual houses, large gardens, and a lake. The townhouse was an end unit, which provided a fireplace. We felt very good about our new life and the challenge of owning our own company. Naturally, I worked for Dick as a sales agent, doing what I did for Pan American, plus handling trips within the United States. I was successful but had to endure much teasing when mispronouncing the various destinations within the United States. The customers played along, thinking that this was part of my accent, but after they had left, there was laughter (Yosemite).

Fortunately, we had inherited the Guy Erway's staff. The travel business was involved. Dick employed the best professional people to guide him, for example, through the intricacies of bookkeeping. There was advertising, developing travels—Dick's specialty—and the brochures describing them. There were the computers and their special programs connecting us with the airlines of the world and the binding contracts. We plugged along; I was often meeting deadlines by driving to the main post office in downtown Baltimore just before midnight to get the airline report stamped with the proper date. This to avoid penalties. When we took a

four year course and obtained our CTC certification, we discovered that we had done things right all along.

Dick was marvelous. He looked so handsome in his well-pressed business suit. Everyone liked him. Such a gentleman. He went over to Charles Street to a bakery to stretch his legs and to pick up something for lunch. "Look what I found," he said, returning with a furry light beige dog cuddled in his arms, still a puppy. "It was hovering at the curb under a car starting to drive away." Well, what to do? We took her home, named her Lucy, and she decided to adopt us. Her fur was blond, long and silky, her eyes dark brown, and her tail, an opulent plume, held proudly in the air. She had a positively motherly attitude toward us, making sure all was well. She came to work with us, sitting on the backseat of the car with  her paws placed on my right shoulder, keeping an eye on traffic. At work, Dick took her for walks. In the Bolton Hill neighborhood, dogs were of the finest lineage. So when Dick was asked what breed of dog Lucy was, he answered, "An African Feather hound." "You see, Edith, when they ask me, I cannot possibly disappoint them by telling them that I am walking a mutt."

All seemed to be normal when one day, a crackling sound was heard. I looked over to where Dick was sitting at his desk and saw the ceiling bulging, then break open with horrible brownish stuff cascading all over him. He did not move a muscle. A major disaster. I screamed, picked up Lucy, and ran out of the office. Obviously, a sewer pipe had broken on top of Dick!

56

Dick asked me whether I would enjoy having my own office. He was negotiating with Johns Hopkins Hospital and School of Medicine to open a travel agency for them. That thought appealed to me.

And that is how I became the manager of the Johns Hopkins branch of the Via Waye Travel Bureau. One of the Hopkins buildings was located across from the hospital, the 550 Building. That is to say, 550 N. Broadway was the address. It was a modern building with a roomy glass-enclosed lobby, doctor's offices above, and apartments for interns and their families. Sheraton had a hotel next door. My business was exclusively for Johns Hopkins travels. I had a direct line into the offices of the physicians and hand-delivered ordered tickets. That is how I lost my way and ended up in the morgue. Oh well.

Being part of the medical team was interesting. Dr. Blizzard sat down at my desk to discuss a trip. He had a needle in his arm and had dark circle under his eyes. "What is happening?" I asked. "I could not get hold of a volunteer," he replied, then went on explaining his travel requirements.

Baltimore prided itself, other than the "Block," on being the home of the Gypsy princess. About ten Gypsies were sitting on the benches in the lobby for support when the princess needed to see a physician.

A world conference was organized by Dr. Arnall Patz, the then director and chief of the ophthalmology department, Johns Hopkins being at the forefront of vision research. I went so far as to pick up three scientists from Dulles airport, who had arrived by the Concorde, a supersonic passenger plane. This superfast jet traveled over the ocean in three hours, rather than the usual seven hours by regular jet. I played the official pick-up service, dressed in a gray plisse skirt, white blouse, and blue blazer with the WAYE logo on it, high heels, and I think I had white gloves on too. My French was good enough to greet them. One professor was drunk. He was overcome by this form of transportation. It was his first time to go faster than Mach 2.

Another conference was organized by the Population Dynamics of the School of Hygiene. I sent tickets to the attendees in Africa, where they were at home.

That became exotic. I was told that there was no postal delivery. Somehow, a box on a tree was mentioned. I am still trying to work that idea out in my mind. Everyone arrived, however, and I had the pleasure of meeting elegant ladies, with their hair braided into a crown, in their long dresses of beautiful designs on the material. They walked in a special way—their heads held up high, very erect and straight, very elegant.

Latin-American customers never ordered anything unless they had impressed on me first that they were personal friends of somebody important at home. It never failed, which makes me understand that in their countries, this is the only way you can get things done.

57

I sat at my desk when I heard a thud against the window; I looked up and saw three young, about eight years old, boys laughing. Then they threw a puppy against the window and scurried away. I went outside to investigate and found a beagle-type puppy on the ground.

Another dog in trouble. We adopted her and called her Priscilla. She was so pretty, large brown eyes, silky long ears. Just one thing—we could not have her in an office setting. She was wild and undisciplined. We did our best to calm her, to no avail. She created mayhem when left alone at home. She was able to eat everything, and she did, and her digestion seemed to take care of whatever came along: nylon stockings, part of the stamp collection, books. A good friend of ours, a federal judge, whose photo had been swallowed by Priscilla, came out again not much worse for wear. It was an incredible joke in our circles. The judge loved it.

I took her to see Dr. Sham on Falls Road, a sensible veterinarian. He looked her over and found a rubber band twisted around her toes and mentioned that her tail had been cut; it was shorter than the typical coonhound he decided she was. He also explained that, just as with humans, dogs could be mentally disturbed as well. "Not a thing you can do about it," he declared. Priscilla could not be trusted at the front door; she wanted out. When she succeeded, we had to chase after her, sometimes by car, with a box of dog bones rattling in our hands, trying to entice her to come back to us.

Mrs. Stout had invited us to dinner. Dick went ahead, with me to follow. Well, Priscilla managed to get out. No way could I catch her; she ran and she ran. At that point, I had had enough. If she was so anxious to leave us, let her go. Mrs. Stout could not be trifled with, and I proceeded to her house. Dick was appalled when I told him of what had happened. He stood up and left to look for her. After quite a while, he returned, and to everyone's surprise, he had found her, way over close to the super Highway 83. She continued to be a curse to our existence. She finally made it to her final destination. When living in Chestertown, she got out and ran into the traffic on Route 20, was hit by a car, and died.

The dogs in our lives. Of course, Lucy continued to be the lady, looking after us and enduring the other dogs.

Johns Hopkins is located in a dangerous neighborhood, and driving to work, I paid attention to the surroundings. Here I was on a heavily traveled road, coming to a stop at a red light when, to my surprise, I saw a little creature trying to cross the road, progressing very slowly—a tiny dog.

The light would change very soon, and trucks were coming from the opposite direction. The dog was so little, the size of a rat almost. Not a chance that a truck would stop for it. While still waiting for the light to change, I jumped out of the car and grabbed the little thing and placed it on the passenger seat. I looked up and saw the driver of the truck next to me smiling and giving me the OK sign. I took this little thing to my office because that is where I was heading and placed it in a cardboard box.

It needed to be washed badly; I noticed many varmints, and from his eyes, brown hardened hair reached down, preventing him to drink or eat.

It was clear that we needed the vet again. He had to shave all his hair off and remove the ticks on his head. He was wearing a dog tag, and I suggested we get in touch with the vet mentioned on it. "No way," said our vet, seeing how he had been mistreated. He found also that that the dog had had distemper at one time. So here was another dog in our life. This was a male, and he looked like a little bare cat, first with many black spots on his head where the tick heads were lodged. His hair began to grow, white and curly. He was a toy poodle. Now we were not small-dog people. Dick grew up with a Saint Bernard. But this little fellow was first, a total male, and secondly, very handsome and smart as is typical of poodles. He lived for three years with us and succumbed to heart disease. His previous life caught up to him. So there we were without a dog. Lucy had died of old age too. A terrible loss for us.

I was asked, "Don't you want another dog?" Following the intense dog experiences of the previous years, I was not too anxious. "The only kind of dog I would enjoy would be a beige toy poodle—but female," I decided. Female because little Reginald had left his marks on all the chair feet, a thing males like to do, to show who is the boss, I learned.

Some years went by, I received a call to announce the birth of toy poodles, beige, and there was a female available. Well, by now, we really wanted a puppy again, and Genevieve Mayerling Foley arrived. She was so small, I was afraid I would step on her. I carried her in the nape of my

neck, holding her there with my left hand while preparing our meals with the right hand. A tiny lined basket stood on my desk in the office with her in it. How wonderful it was. Training her was easy, and she was cuddly and sweet,  and when she was a bit more mature, she loved to run. For part of her exercise routine, I carried a long stick and swung it over the grass; she chased the tip of it.

She went everywhere with us. Later when I had to commute to Baltimore, I bought a little car seat for her. When we started to drive, she curled up in it, and I could reach over to the passenger side and pat her. I had also made a leash for her in beige and extra long to give her the freedom to roam. During office hours in Chestertown, I walked her from Queen Street up High Street to the harbor and back two times a day. We were always stopped for a little chat by friends who sat on their front porch.

58

In Baltimore, my office was in the back, with the desks of the travel agents in the front facing the street. After Dick had died in 1986, I took his place, which necessitated my commuting on weekends and living during the week in the apartment Dick had occupied. The neighborhood there was marginally safe. Once, my car had been broken into by smashing a window and breaking the steering column. So I did not feel safe to walk Genny there at night. We developed a system: I put her on the extra long leash I had crocheted and lifted her out of the back window onto the lawn that reached up because I had a ground-floor apartment. That worked beautifully. She had lots of freedom to roam. Whenever Genny needed to go out, she pointed to the window. Her presence kept me focused after Dick's death. After all, she had been part of us both.

In Baltimore, after Dick had died in 1986 and I took over the agencies, I had placed a soft pillow in a corner of my office where I could see her, and that was her spot. When she heard a voice in the front office that intrigued her, she would get up and walk out to investigate. I usually followed her to make sure that she was not bothering anybody. But there she was, cuddled up on somebody's lap, both customer and dog perfectly happy. Genny lived with me until the ripe old dog age of sixteen. Her little paw imprints on wet paint are still on one of the wooden beams of my porch. She is buried in the woods behind my house here in Chestertown, with a little gravestone.

So far, I covered a time span that stretched into 1986. Previously, I was working as manager of the Johns Hopkins Branch of Via Waye Travel at

550 Broadway, handling the travels of the medical community. That brought interesting persons into my life. My staff: a tiny woman with straight black hair and bangs reaching for her sparkling black eyes. Her ready smile showed her white regular teeth. She was of Mexican descent and a delight to be with. Everybody liked her friendliness and compassion. At lunchtime, she was embroidering in a fashion I had never seen before. She filled in little squares of red checkered material with bright-colored thread. Then there was the lady from India, the elegant wife of an Indian intern. She was beautiful with her oval face and light-colored skin, moving gracefully. I had to get used to her bobbing her head gently from side to side when agreeing with me. It looked more like a negative sign, which surprised me at first. Her family, obviously of some standing, lived in Bombay, and she went to visit them. That is when she contracted a rather serious tropical disease. It took quite a while for her to return to her husband and her job. She was a good friend.

Johns Hopkins Medical Institutions were located in the poorest area of Baltimore, and security was an issue. Driving to work, I made sure the doors of the car were locked. I heard that a doctor had been stabbed in his car. Parking was behind the 550 Building, a fast, short walk to the main entrance. The lobby was glass enclosed, and there was a desk with someone in attendance. Carpeting was light blue, with leather benches along the windows. Our office had its glass door leading into this lobby, with the front wall facing the lobby made of glass also. I had my office enclosed behind the front part with its three desks and a small office to the side, also enclosed, and from there a door lead into the side hallway, very handy. I kept a keen eye on what was happening in the office at all times. Somebody had made it past the front desk; he was obviously out of place, making a nuisance out of himself. So I sneaked out of my office through the side office to alert the desk clerk about our problem, who then would put things in order again by removing the man.

The pressure of becoming a physician overwhelmed some students. Fortunately, we did not witness a student taking his life by jumping out of the window of the dormitory located next to our building. Also, a student collapsed walking into the 550 lobby. He had no idea who he was or where he was. Working thirty-six hours at a stretch, as was part of the routine then, must have been overwhelming.

—

59

This was also where I was during the riots. They happened April 6-9, 1968, just after we had opened our office, with me as the only employee working there. Dick was escorting a group on a cruise as ombudsman, this being our style of service, and I heard about the riot activities on the radio. It turned out that Baltimore was one of the cities most affected. Chaos erupted on the streets, with rampant rioting and looting. Many buildings and structures were burned, as the streets of the inner city became engulfed in flames. Well, I would not allow anything to happen to my new beautiful office at 550 Broadway. I mean, we had just moved the new desk and the chairs there and the filing cabinet. Living in the north of the city, I usually had to drive through the area that was affected by the rioting; I as a white person would not have had a chance. I decided that the way to reach the office was to drive way down to the harbor then east to the Italian neighborhood and then north on Broadway. I arrived safely; when I entered the building, I noticed a car with four black males talking to some young boys. Shortly after that, the Acme food store, a block away, was on fire. It was a very scary time. Martin Luther King had been killed on April 4, and the city was home to a large African American population. SNNC chairman H. Rap Brown was enticing violence with speeches that were a call to arms. The governor established a curfew for all city residents, and the National Guard was called in to quell the riots and restore peace. Life would be different from then on.

60

The travel products we sold were top of the line, and we had to show good taste to the outside world. Dick's clothing was conservative and stylish. We purchased his suits from a factory called Joseph Banks where the tailors made any adjustments necessary, and the price was reasonable. It was an insider's address, and the diplomats from Washington would purchase their suits there too. His shoes came from Miller Brothers on Baltimore Street, right around the corner from Charles and cost $350, an incredible expense for that time.

My wardrobe was self-made. I learned how to sew out of necessity. Dick brought rich-colored hand-loomed woolens from the Moiarity store in Donegal, Ireland, which inspired me to make my own suits. I made my own evening gowns too. I made bedroom curtains by cutting a sheet in half almost to the top where the flowered part became the overhang. Now the seam is sewn together again, and the sheets are still around.

61

Well, there I was, Dick was escorting a group to an exotic destination again. This activity was our moneymaker, and I understood. I was left with the management of the offices and felt left out and tired. Today, we would call it "burn out."

Out front stood the shiny dark green Buick we had purchased from our relative in Augusta, Georgia. We had worked our way up from the smallest Buick to the largest by exchanging each type at Christmas when we were visiting. That was considered a smart thing to do with financial advantages. But now, there it beckoned for me to roam. I simply had to get away. I packed Lucy into the car with a blanket, a pillow, a can opener, dog food, water and a can of beans. That was that, we drove to Colonial Williamsburg without a reservation at a hotel, nor did I have any money other than my household cash. It was wonderful; I took an interesting tour of the colonial town. Before I knew it, it was evening. Well, I had to be safe and looked for a place to park the car. The motel, part of the Williamsburg accommodation, was my choice. There were plenty of open spaces right at the doors to each unit, and I parked the car in one of them. Of course, we had to be invisible in the car. I talked to Lucy to be very still and not to bark, even when she heard persons outside. She was typically wonderful. She understood, and the two of us huddled under the blanket and had a peaceful sleep.

This was the time before credit cards and cell phones, before home computers and spending money one did not have. Dick's well-to-do family had lost all during the Depression—the estate in Pennsylvania, the private railroad car, the butler, and chauffeur with the Perciera car—and I had lost all dear to me during World War II. To us, making money was a sport and a necessity, working our way back to what we knew and grew up with.

62

Our comfortable townhouse in Ruxton was a rental. Not a good financial situation. The rental money should build equity, and a house needed to be bought. We looked in Ruxton and saw a place we would enjoy to live in, but it was in such bad shape that the outlay was too high. The mortgage available from banks was geared toward how much regular income one had, a certain percentage. The houses in Ruxton were really not a good investment for us. They were priced for their location, and old. We found a house at a dead-end, with the watershed woods behind it called Dogwood Hill Court just off the end of Providence Road. It was roomy and light, and we decided that this was going to be our new home. The neighbors were delightful, and we had much fun visiting with them and enjoying their hospitality; the door was always open. At the back of our house, on the ground floor, was a terrace, and that is where we held many a dinner party, and all was well. A friend called; he was moving back to England and was selling his furniture. That is were we bought items to fill our new home and felt that two Persian rugs would be appropriate, and we found a reliable firm. What an experience to see Mr. Hanna flip through the high pile of rugs to see what type we would like. The red Heriz was easily decided on for the dining room, but the large one for the living room area was so pink. We were intrigued but unsure. "You may live with it for a while to see whether you like it," suggested Mr. Hanna, and that is what we did. The rug is still with me and represents many other colors together, with the pink a joy to behold. Also, we felt that the business would be more effective in a neighborhood where most of our clientele was located and moved to Roland Park, to the second floor of a small mall on Roland Avenue. The business was going well. Dick's style was appreciated.

Mutti and Micaela came to visit. Micaela was working in Washington at the time because her friend had a position there.

63

It was 1952. Dick had just left home to escort a group when a hurricane struck. The rain was intense. A curtain, dense like a sheet of water, came down for days. Our street descending toward our house became a river. The foundation of our house could not withstand the pressure and let the water in. The basement, together with one room downstairs, filled with water. I think it receded finally by itself. We did not have central air-conditioning, and the house began to smell. Mildew! We lived with that for a while because on the floor above was the living and sleeping area, but we decided to purchase a house on Providence Road, a house so beautiful in a large garden richly landscaped. My dream house! It was a lot of work to sell the house on Dogwood Hill Court after the water damage. We had to get rid of mildewed rugs and upholstered furniture. The cellar walls had to be waterproofed with a special paint, and I hid Yardley's lavender soap wherever possible to give the house a fresh smell. Of course, I did all of that myself. I loved a challenge. We needed to sell the place.

Other things were happening. Dick's office in Roland Park became too small. We needed to hire more personnel. A popular area north of Baltimore was Towson. Traditionally, Baltimore residents would have summer residences there to get out of the heat of the Baltimore bowl. Towson was elevated and caught cooling breezes. It began to develop with many lovely homes, and then an extensive mall was built. We decided that we would be effective there and relocated to the Towson Mall.

After a successful year or so, Dick had an idea, which I did not support. Next door to the travel agency was a large space, which he rented, and a travel boutique was developed. The display shelves arrived; they were beautiful in their elegance and simplicity. A person was hired to be the manager. I did not like her. Some items to be sold began to arrive. Then suddenly, the economy began to falter. The stock market plunged. It was 1973. There were long lines at gas stations to get gasoline, and the truckers struck nationwide. Our boutique was waiting for merchandise that did not arrive because of the truckers' strike and stayed mostly empty, and it was time for Christmas shopping.

Nobody was traveling. The management of the mall, all with Italian names from New York, was merciless in requiring the rent. What to do? The business was our livelihood and had to survive. We decided to sell the dream house, and the small business administration lent us $70,000. It helped to have a good reputation. We always had placed any profit back into the business. That included increases in staff salary and their insurances. We left the Towson Mall and moved to

a small mall across the street owned by a good Jewish family who were very helpful, and that is where the office still strives.

After the sale of the dream house, a house was rented in a pleasant established neighborhood off York Road, 818 Stoneleigh Road.

After seven years, Dick paid off the $70,000 loan. He was working in Towson, and I at the Johns Hopkins office. I drove a small beige secondhand car and did not feel well after driving it for a while. What did I know, the muffler had a leak, and I was breathing pure exhaust. I think once in a while, I hung my head out the window. But I was not going to complain. It was finally fixed, of course.

Several alumni from Washington College, Chestertown, lived in the Baltimore area. The Christmas party of the Baltimore branch of the Washington College Alumni Association was traditionally held at our house. I enjoyed decorating for this occasion. It put us in the mood for Christmas too. I prepared the food to be served, and Dick handled the drinks. About eight or ten persons participated. The fire was roaring in the fireplace. The alumni, with their spouses, had a good time remembering their lives and adventures at the college. It had started to snow heavily once, and it was not easy to make it out of the driveway. But everyone made it. Anne Burris lives now in Kennedyville, and Gail and Charles Waesche, who lived on Charles Street in Towson, have moved to Rock Hall.

My back gave me a bad problem. I do not remember what brought it on, but it was so bad that I had to climb the stairs to the second floor on my hands and knees, up and down. To empty the dishwasher, I was lying on the floor, could not bend at all. I am mentioning this because that made it clear to me that one should, at a later date in life, be prepared and live in a one-floor house. I was fitted with a device, the word corset sort of does not sound nice, with metal bars supporting the spine and the ribcage in front. That gave the spine time to heal, and it did. The fact that I had to wear it for six months and that it was summertime left an impression.

64

Someone wanted to buy my business. The man was our accountant, his wife a teacher soon to be retired, and my agency seemed to be a good investment for them. Dick was intrigued. The place where he grew up always had a pull. His sister Birdie Ellen Virginia Richards, the one we visited every year in Augusta, Georgia, had lost her husband Cherry, sold the Buick Agency, and moved in 1975 back to Chestertown. The family had lived in the what we call now the Miller House on Water Street, and Birdie found a house two doors down on the river and moved in. I was there to help her. A sweet voice was calling from the open door, "I hear that pretty Birdie Foley is back." That was Chestertown. Everybody knew each other well. The front doors were always open, and one could see through the living and dining room and the river room out to the Chester River. There was always a gentle breeze moving through the house.

We had cocktails on the porch overlooking the river, and the neighbors greeted each other sitting on their porches. Roses liked the nearness of the river and bloomed in profusion in her river garden. The neighbor Bob

Bryan had worked for DuPont and had all the right chemicals to help the flowers along.

On the Fourth of July, the family was invited and crabs were consumed. Lots of beer helped the efforts along, and baked beans and potato salad and that sort of thing was offered to provide some substance to the meal. Susanne and Linda and Johnny were there, Birdie's children and, later, Lara and Chip, Susanne's children. We were a handsome and happy group sitting under the porch

at the river's edge, with newspapers on the table where the crabs were placed for their consumption after a rather complicated way of retrieving some meat from their innards.

Dick asked me, "Would you be interested to move to Chestertown?" I knew that it meant the world to him. He considered Chestertown his real home. After our relationship took on a serious turn in 1962, he took me to Chestertown to see whether I could belong there. I was used to small towns in Holland and liked the place, although at that time, the town was sleepy and not in good shape.

The plans began to take shape. The sale of my office would enable us to purchase a home in Chestertown.

David Barroll took as around. I had specified "No dead-end, not in the woods, please." We saw several places. "Where do you think we should live, David?" I asked, not knowing the lay of the land and where who lived. He showed us a very nice place in town. Dick did not like it; he preferred the country. So where did we end up? On a dead-end street in the woods surrounded by cornfields and Canadian geese, about two and a half miles south of town.

The house had been built for Alex Rasin and his family, which was a recommendation. We knew the family well and trusted Alex, who was a lawyer and still is. We managed to buy it at a reasonable price. The Rasins, then having small children, wanted to be closer to town to cut down commuting time. Mr. Fiorilli, on the corner of Franklin and Calvert Street in Baltimore, recovered some of our chairs with raw silk.

The house has three bedrooms, two full baths, a living room with fireplace, dining room, kitchen, den, and a porch at the front entrance. All doors are made of sturdy solid wood. This was good. The furniture fit well, just the dining room's red Heriz clashed with the yellow wallpaper and curtains. That design had brown nests on it, with crocuses and their roots. Later I changed all that.

65

I knew Mr. Wilbur Hubbard. He was the richest man in town, living at Wide Hall on the river on the end of High Street. He was of small stature, with a benign round face and sparse blond hair. Horses were the center of his life. He owned several, stabled  on Airy Hill Road across from Brownie's house. Brownie looked after his horses and the forty-some hounds who lived next to his house.

 Wilbur was a master of the hunt. What a delight it was to see him and his friends galloping through the fields, jumping over hedges dressed in their what is known as "pinks," but actually were bright-red jackets. They followed on their horses, the baying forty hounds that were in hot pursuit of a fox. Well, you may have seen the English prints of a fox chase. This was just like it, wonderful to see. Later he was the oldest master of the hunt in his nineties.

I had the experience of dancing with him at a hunt party in Monkton, the Baltimore horsey area. The top of his head reached just under my chin.

He was not married and never would. A man lived with him, considered to be his butler type.

I attended a meeting of the Chestertown Historical Society where Wilbur gave a talk about his growing up in Chesterton. His experiences reached way back into the time of his parent's life, a wonderful picture about what Chestertown was like. I had heard from Dick that Chestertown was a busy Maryland harbor, even before Baltimore.

Wilbur, whose parents owned a fertilizer company, explains that the railroad played an important role. There were no cars and no streets in town, just dirt roads with ditches to carry off the rainwater. The farms produced peaches in abundance until blight killed the trees. The wheat farming was done by hand and horsepower. The threshing with the one machine around was a community effort. The resulting straw inspired a cardboard factory on the corner of High Street and the bypass.

He remembered well when the first horseless carriages were brought to Chestertown from Baltimore on the Chester River steamboat, which landed at the foot of High Street about 7:00 PM in late spring, about 1903 or '04. They were pushed off the steamboat, cranked up, and after spitting and sputtering a bit, they went *chug chug chug* up High Street with a crowd of boys following and shouting with glee.

This curious contraption was then called by most people a horseless carriage, and it literally looked like a buggy without the horse. It had high wheels with wooden spokes and little narrow rubber tires like those on expensive carriages. There was a dashboard like a buggy, but no windshield and no steering wheel—only a rod with which to steer. It was a single-seated vehicle. The motor was under the seat with a crank on the side. There was a sprocket wheel from the motor and a chain drive to the rear wheels nearby.

Another worthwhile part of Wilbur's presentation concerns the history of the Vickers family. There is a historical marker right near the telephone office on Washington Avenue about Senator George Vickers, who was a very prominent political figure in the middle of the nineteenth century. He was born in 1801, nearly sixty years old at the outbreak of the Civil War. He opposed secession for Maryland in 1861. He assisted Governor Hicks in raising an Eastern Shore regiment and attained the rank of major general in the militia. The son of this man became a lawyer living on High Street, also interested in local politics.

"Mr. Vickers," a man asked him, "could you please lend me $5? I will pay you back on Saturday." Well, in those days, $5 was quite an amount of money, and he thought that he might not be repaid. He, however, wanted the man's goodwill for political reasons. To his surprise, the man came in on Saturday and repaid the $5. "That is a lucky $5. I am going to send it to the Louisiana Lottery." It turned out that it was the winning ticket, and Mr. Vickers won $75,000. He went to New Orleans to collect.

Mr. Vickers was an ardent Methodist. In those days, the Methodists thought it was sinful to drink, gamble, and dance. Mrs. Vickers did not want her husband to refuse the money, but she was so embarrassed, she would not admit that it was acquired by gambling. She and her daughters would never talk about it, not even to their children. Mr. Vickers was not as churchly as his wife. The Methodist preacher came to him and said, "This money you have won is tainted money. You should redeem yourself with the Lord by making a large contribution to the church."

Mr. Vickers replied, "You think this money is so tainted, I will relieve your conscience. I won't contaminate you or the church. I won't give you or the church one damn red cent."

This is the atmosphere I felt when Chestertown became my home. Dick had grown up here on the river on Water Street as a boy, and I was becoming a part of it. Mentioning to his contemporaries "I am Dickie Foley's wife," I was met with an understanding smile of recognition.

The time, driving over the Chester River bridge, when it became clear that Chestertown was going to be my new home, I happily felt that I had arrived in my life, leaving behind all that had been in the past, and recently, the hard work at my travel agency on Broadway in Baltimore. I felt the peace of this small old town on the river. It filled me with joy. I had survived.

Get Published, Inc!
Thorofare, NJ 08086
22 October 2009
BA2009235